Hope Deferred Makes the Heart Sick
But When the Desire Comes It is a Tree of Life

Dewhitt L. Bingham

Jerry,

Thanks for your Support! May God bless everything you put your hands to do. - Dewhitt

Copyright © 2017 by Dewhitt L. Bingham

All rights reserved.

No part of this book may be reproduced, in any form, without written permission from the publisher.

Request for permission to reproduce selections from this book should be mailed to the publisher.

ISBN: 978-0-692-84087-0

Printed in the United States of America

Cover photo taken by Audrey Stickrod, Courtesy of Heartland Community College. Photos edited by Jenny Crones. Book edited by Anne Colloton. Cover photo of Heartland Community College's Male Empowerment Network Club's annual Domestic Violence Event. Cover arranged by Gwenda Sutton and Dewhitt Bingham.

In remembrance of Warren and Anna Mae Bingham, Clara Casey, Verena Robinson, Jeannette Mosby, Clarence Kaiser, Eddie Mosby, Erlis Porter, Larry, Paul (Jr.) and James Hall, Ralph Bingham, and Adrian Blevins.

Contents

Introduction	1
Chapter 1: Hope Deferred Makes the Heart Sick	8
Chapter 2: The Desires of the Heart	18
Chapter 3: What You Hope'n For	27
Chapter 4: Heavenly Conversation	32
Chapter 5: Building Bridges with Love	42
Chapter 6: The Law of Reciprocity	51
Chapter 7: Take Fast Hold of Instructions	59
Chapter 8: Joy Cometh in the Morning	68
Chapter 9: Be a Giver Not a Taker	75
Chapter 10: For the Love of Money	83
Chapter 11: Put a Ring on It	92
Chapter 12: These Three Words	98
Chapter 13: Things	104

Chapter 14:	Can Anything Good Come Out of Nazareth	112
Chapter 15:	Muzzle Not the Ox	121
Chapter 16:	Throwing Stones	132
Chapter 17:	Reserving the Right	140
Chapter 18:	Second Chance	149
Chapter 19:	A Church without Spot or Wrinkle	159
Chapter 20:	Jesus the Same Yesterday Today and Evermore	165
Chapter 21:	Cut It Off	175
Chapter 22:	Bewitched	183
Chapter 23:	Temptation a Promise	191
Chapter 24:	Judgment Day	199
Chapter 25:	Can You Take It	207
Chapter 26:	Standing in the Gap	216
Chapter 27:	The Death Penalty	223

Chapter 28: Have You Heard	232
Chapter 29: A Form of Godliness	241
Chapter 30: Power Connection	250
Conclusion	258

Acknowledgments

I want to thank God for sending his only begotten son, Jesus Christ, to die on the cross for me. Jesus is king of kings and Lord of Lords. Greater love hath no man than this that a man lay down his life for a friend. When I was sinking away in sin, God saw fit to send Jesus to die for me that I might have life and life more abundantly. Great is the Lord and he is greatly to be praised, in the city of our God and in the mountain of his holiness. I thank him for allowing me the privilege to enter into his gates with thanksgiving and into his courts with praise on a daily basis. I understand that he is the reason I live, move, and have my being, and cannot go under for going over, for greater is he that is in me than he that is in the world. I thank him for his promises, that I am the salt of the earth, a light that sits on a hill that cannot be hidden, a peculiar person, who is very special to him. I am committed to letting my light shine until either he calls me home or the rapture takes place.

Though my mother gave birth to me at the young age of sixteen, God knew me before I was even formed in her womb, but surely she wondered how she would raise this New Year's baby born on January 1, 1962 in the midst of a rapidly changing world. Annette Hall, I love you. You could have aborted me, but you didn't. Just as Christ beautifies the meek with salvation, you beautified me with your love, long suffering, kind and compassionate genes. God made me just like you and it is my dream to someday marry a woman that is as beautiful as you. You are the best mother on God's green earth.

Paul Hall Sr., you are all that and much more. I so appreciate you for taking care of me and all my siblings. I long for the early years when we use to go to Smitty's for a hamburger. Even though times were hard, we ate in shifts, and very seldom had seconds, you made sure we never missed a meal and for that I love you so much. God blessed you to be an awesome provider.

To my siblings, Paula (Peaches) Hall, Wanda Henderson, Tammy Bingham, Janice Jones, Cara Blevins, and Galen Hall, I love you to death. I could not have asked for greater siblings than you. God says honor thy mother and father that you may have long life. I really appreciate how you guys have always been there for Mom and Paul, when I haven't because of my career. You guys are awesome.

To my Aunts Vera, Janette, Pricilla, and my uncle Stanley, I so appreciate you for all that you did for me as I was growing up. As is often said, it takes a village to raise a child. I thank you for the love you gave and are still giving to me. There isn't a greater core of aunts and uncle on God's green earth. I could not have fared better if I'd handpicked you myself; you are truly a blessing from God.

To all my many cousins, relatives and friends who were a part of my life growing up, made life worth living, and encouraged me along this journey of life, I say thank you. Each of you has been a blessing to me. Whether you are a first, second or third cousin, niece, nephew or grandchild, friend to me and my family, a high school classmate, or God put you in my path while in college, you have been a blessing in my life and I will never forget it.

Finally, to my Pastors Vicky and Joseph Brown and my church family, I want to say thank you for being my family away from home. Together we are doing a work for God and building something that will last throughout eternity. The word of God says that heaven and earth are going to pass away, but his word is going to last forever, the grass withereth the flower fadeth, but the word of God is going to last eternally. You've taught me that only what I do for Christ is going to last and you are truly the righteousness of God. I love you all.

Introduction

After accepting Christ as my Lord and savior in September of 1985 I began to live my life according to God's word and I could see the positive change in my attitude, beliefs and behavior. As a Christian and while serving as the head Elder of Integrity Deliverance Ministry I've learned that for every natural question and situation there is a spiritual answer and solution. Throughout the past thirty years of my life I certainly have not been perfect and made many mistakes, but I've done my best to govern my life according to God's principles and precepts. I am so grateful for God's forgiving power and how his word says that if we fall we have an advocate with the Father. I thank him for his grace and mercy following me every day. Whether I'm preaching the word of God, teaching and training my two young adult children, doing my job as Probation Officer, teaching students as an Adjunct Professor at Heartland Community College, or doing any other human endeavor, I always try to allow Christ to guide me.

As a criminal justice practitioner for the past 30 years, the police shootings of unarmed African American men and the police killings have been more than disturbing and are the primary motivating factors for this book. Whether white on white crime, black on black crime, murder, or mistreatment of another, I believe it is a result of a lack of hope. I am firmly convinced that when someone purposefully abuses a person or intentionally causes their death, I believe the loss of hope or never having gained it is a major contributor. I'm not just talking about hope as it is defined by Webster, to anticipate, expect or to wish something, but I'm talking about the hope of God. The Bible says that hope deferred makes the heart sick, but when the desire comes it is a tree of life. To understand the aforementioned scripture, I always like to correlate it with the word of God that says a living dog is better than a dead lion. As robust as the lion is, he can do nothing to the dog because he's dead. Unlike the lion, the dog still has an opportunity to receive the hope of God. So it is with us humans, as long as we are breathing we have the opportunity to allow God to change our life. When you have the hope of Christ, you have life and life more abundantly. As a result, you can love those who seem unloving, respect the down trodden, and embrace people who do not look like you.

I am the father of two beautiful twenty-two year old young adult twins. As a father I've always governed myself according to God's word that says train up a child in the way that he should go and when he is old he will not depart from it. With all the hate for the different races being expressed by adults, I am really concerned about the safety and security of our children. My love for Jesus Christ has driven me to teach my children to seek after the hope of God. As a result, I firmly believe they will better understand the feelings of others, have unconditional love, and take a stand against the mistreatment of others.

I too believe that various stereotypes we have learned and internalized about groups other than our own causes fear, confusion, and anger that is sometimes expressed in an evil way toward those groups. Everything we learn is internalized, forming a literal record inside us. Even when our thoughts refute these records, they still exist and can influence our behavior in negative ways. None of us are born with a murderous spirit and we don't want to be prejudicial toward others, but we are taught prejudice, bigotry, and discrimination. We should welcome the opportunity to learn how to be inclusive, tolerant and fair. All groups of people and issues are important when it comes to welcoming diversity, and the hope of God can solve this problem.

Most of the time when we think of prejudicial people, thoughts or behavior, we think of stereotypes a person has about groups other than their own, but the concept of internalized oppression teaches that one of the most painful results of discrimination is a result of internalizing these stereotypes. Internalization of these stereotypes can lead to internalized oppression and become a driving force behind mistreatment of our own group. Many of the things we can't stand about our own groups are internalizations of what people from outside our groups have said about us. In truth, the things we hate about our own groups are scars our groups carry from being mistreated. Through the hope of Christ, we can build greater unity with our own groups which will propel us to build greater unity with all other groups.

As a college professor I work hard to prepare my students to become professional practitioners with a big emphasis on not being a respecter of person and to always treat people with respect. The reason I do this is because perceived stereotypes of African American men by the police is a big contributor to how police treat black men. Likewise, prejudice toward police has caused African Americans to despise our first responders. The National Coalition Building Institute suggests that guilt is the glue that holds prejudice and stereotypes in place.[32] Therefore, with the hope of Christ, public and police knowledge of diversity, along with community policing, the problem can be diminished.

With the hope of Christ you can learn how to take pride in the person you are, speak what you are most proud of about yourself, and what you love about being you without being divisive or derogatory toward others. What I love about African American men is they are strong, professional, and loving. With the hope of Christ, I can resist the stereotypes that others have about my group and not internalize them causing me to be less than fully proud of African Americans. What I love about Police Officers is they are kind, professional, considerate, and they serve and protect the community. If a person is ashamed to say it's great to be a member of a group they are less than proud of, it does nothing to end discrimination. For example, white people who are ashamed of being white because of slavery are not especially helpful in ending racism. This is why if I were to give a speech on civil rights, the first people I would mention is Caucasian heroes of the civil rights movement.

I was compelled to write this book because it is imperative that we put our trust in the Lord, understand that we have similarities and differences, proclaim that every group counts, and declare that every group is important in American society. This book is composed of thirty of the many sermons I have preached on a given Sunday since I accepted Christ as my Lord and Savior. I hope and pray that if you don't have the hope of Christ or if you have withdrawn yourself from Him, you will be compelled to recommit your life. If you already know the Lord and are in good standing with him, I pray that the hope of Christ encourages you to engage in the fight for righteousness even more. God has a purpose for each and every one of our lives and he desires for us to accomplish it.

Chapter 1
Hope Deferred Makes the Heart Sick

There are the Republican and Democratic parties, racial division, social injustice, economic stagnation, white supremacy, and Black Lives Matter. Occasionally it feels like a ticking time bomb about to explode or a revolution is about to take place. So, we definitely need the Lord.

In her book *My Beloved World*, Justice Sonia Sotomayor, the first Hispanic Supreme Court Justice states, "The dream I first followed was to become a judge, which itself seemed far-fetched until it actually happened. The idea of my becoming a Supreme Court Justice, which, indeed, as a goal would inevitably elude the vast majority of aspirants, never occurred to me except as the remotest of fantasies. But experience has taught me that you cannot value dreams according to the odds of their coming true. Their real value is in stirring within us the will to aspire."

Justice Sotomayor would wake up to her father yelling and knew in just a few minutes she would hear her mother

Hope Deferred Makes the Heart Sick

Salina screaming at her father, Juan Luis, affectionately called Juli. Salina would say, "Juli you're going to have to learn how to do it because I'm not going to be here all the time." Meaning, Juli would have to learn how to give Justice Sotomayor an insulin shot. Yes, Justice Sotomayor found out she had diabetes at the age of eight. Her father would die when she was nine years old; he drank himself to death.

Justice Sotomayor walks up to both of her parents, grabs the syringe and the needle and throws it in some boiling water. Salina begins to ask, "Sonia do you know what you are doing? You have to make sure the needle is sterile and it has to be free from bacteria." Justice Sotomayor tells her parents, "I'm going to give it." Then she says, "Why am I saying that I'm going to give it when I'm actually getting it? I'm going to give it and get it" referring to administering insulin to herself at the age of eight.

To find a woman with hope, look no further than Salina Sotomayor who lost her mother at a very young age. In

Hope Deferred Makes the Heart Sick 1944 she altered her birth certificate to read nineteen years of age when she was really seventeen, jumped a train from Puerto Rico to New York, and entered the Women's Army Corp. Between the years of 1940 and 1945 approximately two hundred Puerto Rican bilingual women were trained to be interpreters, cryptologists, and communication specialists. Salina Sotomayor is a woman who had hope and was determined to have a better life.

Justice Sotomayor goes on to tell about how she went to Catholic school and how the school priest refused to pray for her mother because Salina did not attend church on a regular basis. However, the priest always accepted the offering given by Justice Sotomayor every Sunday. This offering of course would be given to Justice Sotomayor by her mother Salina. The Sotomayor family lived in the Bronx and was very poor.

Justice Sotomayor also tells about how she received a card in the mail letting her know that she was a candidate for Princeton University. Her high school nurse asked her

Hope Deferred Makes the Heart Sick

why she got a possible and the number one and two students in the class did not. All this gave her hope. She continues to be fueled by that look the nurse gave her and the questioning if she was good enough to attend Princeton.[37]

The word of God states that a living dog is better than a dead lion. Meaning, as long as you are alive you have a chance to be joined to a living thing. That living thing is Jesus Christ. There are good times and bad times in our lives. The key issues are twofold: bad things happen to everyone eventually, good times can be created, involve achievement and the sharing of that accomplishment with others.[30] I don't know about you, but I choose to live, have life and be joined to the hope of Christ.

Hope is defined as having expectation, optimism, and anticipation. It is correlated with salvation in that you cannot have one without the other. We are saved by grace, but receive salvation through faith. Faith is the substance of things hoped for and the evidence of things not seen.

Hope Deferred Makes the Heart Sick

So, you cannot have the faith it takes to receive grace that saves you if you don't have hope. What am I saying? When this hope is deferred the heart becomes sick and there is a direct relationship between evil and hateful behavior and the lack of hope.

God said he knew you before you were formed in the womb and made you especially for his purpose. You are the salt of the earth, light of the world, and according to Peter 2:9, a peculiar person. He said you are like a light that sits upon a hill that cannot be hidden and you are fearfully and wonderfully made. You are somebody special.

For proof look no further than the body of man. It houses two hundred and sixty-three bones, six hundred muscles, thirty-two feet of intestines, nine hundred and seventy miles of blood vessels, thirty pounds of blood, which makes a complete circuit every two minutes. In that body of yours is the heart. The heart is four by six inches in size, beats seventy-two times a minute, four thousand two

Hope Deferred Makes the Heart Sick

hundred times an hour. In addition, this same body has a soul and spirit.[14]

The soul and spirit formulate and the body executes. What is the soul and spirit? The soul is the seat of your affections, emotions and desires. The spirit can be viewed as your intellect, mind and conscious. Inordinate affections, emotions, and desires come because of a lack of hope. An unstable intellect, mind or conscious results from hopelessness. Herein is why people are often depressed, neurotic, or even psychotic. My prayer is that God blesses those with organic mental illness, but many people suffer from mental illness as a result of trying to live this life on their own. This body was not made to function without God.

As for Black Lives Matter, it is not a terrorist group. Hope deferred is not why we have BLM. It exists because there is hope that police officers will stop killing black men. Please do not say to me every time an unarmed black man is killed by a police officer, I should speak out when there

Hope Deferred Makes the Heart Sick is black on black crime, black people commit most of the crime, are arrested more often and are killed because of the opportunity created because they commit more crime.

On the contrary, here are the facts. In 2014, for murder where there was a single victim and single offender, there was approximately 2500 white on white murders and approximately 2200 black on black murders. Sixty-nine percent of people arrested were white and twenty-seven point eight percent were black. We have Black on Black crime, but we also have White on White crime. A 2016 study by the Center for Policing Equity found that blacks were targeted more and according to Justin Nix of the University of Louisville, high crime neighborhoods had nothing to do with police shootings. It had more to do with the perceived threat and stereotypes of black people.[29]

Hope deferred makes you commit illegal searches and have an illegal stop and frisk policy. Look no further than Floyd v. the City of New York City. While the police argued that it saved lives, Judge Shira Scheindlin ruled

Hope Deferred Makes the Heart Sick that officers were quick to deem suspicion, stopped people without an objective reason of suspected wrongdoing, and that black stops had a lesser degree of suspicion than whites. She called it the human toll of unconstitutional stops.

From 2004 to 2012 there were 4.5 million stops. Eighty-three percent of the people stopped were African American or Hispanic. Ninety percent of the people stopped resulted in no arrest. Judge Scheindlin ruled that African Americans and Hispanics were viewed as the right people to stop while high officials and commanders turned their head. Officers stopped people for minor things such as having a cell phone, carrying a wallet, grabbing at their pocket, being fidgety, changing directions, walking a certain way, and looking over their shoulder.

As a result of the indirect racial profiling found in the Floyd Case, the New York Police Department has been ordered to wear body cameras and reform with public input. The District Attorney was ordered to monitor it all,

Hope Deferred Makes the Heart Sick

and if the behavior does not change, the court has said disciplinary action will be taken against those officers who make illegal Terry Stops.[21]

Hope deferred makes the heart sick, but when the desire comes, it is a tree of life. Desire is defined as a want to, wish, longing for or a want, wish and longing to do the right thing. This person respects, stands in awe of, reverences, pleases and fears the commandments of God. There is a tree of life in heaven and it is for the healing of the nation. When the desire has come, police and civilians will have a heart similar to that of the Wichita Police Department and Black Lives Matter civilians in the state of Oklahoma. Instead of looking to kill each other, a protest turned into a BBQ. Protesters met with police, and officers stated "we need to see individuals as people." After the picnic was over it became a forum.[45]

Come on America we can do this. Let us have the hope of Noah who did all that God commanded him to do, proclaim the hope of Job whose life and resolve was tested

Hope Deferred Makes the Heart Sick beyond imagination, yet he did not curse God, have the hope of Ruth who said to Naomi, "Entreat me not to leave thee, for where you go I will go, and where you lodge I will lodge," and have the hope of Joseph who was devoted to the Lord even in times of injustice, betrayal and temptation.

Chapter 2
The Desires of Your Heart

In March of 2008, the Huffington Post released a recording from Pastor John Hagee's sermon that stated, "God says in Jeremiah 16: Behold, I will bring them the Jewish people again unto their land that I gave to their fathers. Behold, I will send for many fishers, and after will I send for many hunters. And they the hunters shall hunt them." That would be the Jews. Then God sent a hunter. A hunter is someone who comes with a gun and he forces you. Hitler was a hunter.

In regard to the aforementioned statement, Senator John McCain said, "Obviously, I find these remarks and others deeply offensive and indefensible, and I repudiate them. I did not know of them before Reverend Hagee's endorsement, and I feel I must reject his endorsement as well." Reverend Hagee stated, "I am tired of these baseless attacks and fear that they have become a distraction in what should be a national debate about important issues. I have therefore decided to withdraw my endorsement of

The Desires of Your Heart

Senator McCain for president effective today and to remove myself from any active role in the 2008 campaign."

Senator McCain also said that his relationship with Reverend Hagee did not compare with Obama's lengthy association with the Reverend Jeremiah Wright. But, the Arizona senator previously renounced comments from Hagee that termed the Catholic Church "the great whore" and "an apostate church."

In a statement released before McCain rejected his endorsement, Reverend Hagee said his words had been taken out of context. Hagee stated, "The intentional mischaracterization of my statements by an Internet journalist seeking to use me as a political football in the upcoming presidential race is a gross example of bias at its worst. I will not stand idly by while my character is assassinated and my views on the Holocaust are grossly distorted. To assert that I in any way condone the Holocaust or that monster, Adolf Hitler, is the biggest and

The Desires of Your Heart

ugliest of lies. I have always condemned the horrors of the Holocaust in the strongest of terms."

It was also implied that Reverend Hagee blamed Katrina on gays in New Orleans and that Islam has a biblical mandate to kill Christians and Jews. "The notion that the Holocaust was part of God's plan as a way of punishing the Jews is a deeply, deeply troubling assertion to be repudiated by all people of conscience," said Rabbi David Saperstein of the Religious Action Center of Reform Judaism.

As reported by CNN, Senator McCain also faced similar pressure to distance himself from the Reverend Rod Parsley over the minister's statement that Islam was an antichrist religion that intends through violence to conquer the world. As a result, Senator McCain had to reject Parsley's remarks and his endorsement.[48]

There cannot be a double standard. Everyone counts and all issues regarding every race and ethnicity matters.

The Desires of Your Heart

Whether you are John McCain, President Obama, Pastor Jeremiah Wright, Hagee or Parsley, we as Americans should have respect of person and no one should be exempt from constructive criticism. When mistakes are made, we which are spiritual should restore such a one. Jesus prayed that we would not be selfish, self centered, and arrogant.

There is something to be said about the desires of men and women. The things that people strive after never cease to amaze me. We need to examine ourselves everyday to make sure we have the best interest of all people. We have to ask ourselves what are our desires and what should we be pursuing. We can't expect to hear the Lord say enter and well done, good and faithful servant if our desires are mean spirited. We cannot be in the service of Jesus Christ for the fishes and the loaves.

Many don't understand the importance of the heart as it relates to happiness. The desires of the heart are important for many reasons and the Bible is plain about this. The

The Desires of Your Heart

Bible clearly informs us that from the abundance of the heart the mouth speaks, out of the heart proceeds evil thoughts, murders, adulteries, fornications, thefts, false witness, and blasphemies. If a person's heart has been changed from sinfulness to righteousness, one will not be a murderer, thief or a whore. Don't tell me your heart is right and you are murdering people with your tongue.

Murder is the intentional killing of one person by another. Adultery is having sexual intercourse with another man's wife or another woman's husband. Fornication is premarital sex or sexual intercourse with someone that you are not married to. Stealing is taking or carrying away with intent to deprive someone of their property. This all takes place because of the state of the heart. This is why scripture proclaims that it is not good enough to confess with the mouth, but you also have to believe in your heart. For with the heart man believeth unto righteousness, and with the whole heart is how we should love God till death.

The Desires of Your Heart

God knows that where our treasure is there will our heart be also. Subsequently, without a changed heart it is impossible to be your brother's keeper, sell your possessions and give to the poor or respect all races of people. David said the righteous need not be upset or irritated by the prosperity of the wicked for it is temporary and therefore should be undesirable.

I have lived long enough to experience how each race has disrespected and mistreated races other than their own, but in order to be a bridge builder you have to believe that the prosperity of the wicked will fade and love will abound in the end. The word of God makes it known that evil behavior separates us from righteousness and will cause God to say "Depart from me you worker of iniquity." This caused David, a man after God's own heart to say, "Think it not strange that evil people prosper; it happened in my day and it will happen in times to come." He implies that the Christian should not be jealous of the world but desire to shake the restraints of this perception. This belief is the driving force behind being able to love your brother and not mistreat him. In addition, it is what can unify and unite people for the common good. God wants the world to be saved.

Whether a black civilian assassinates a police officer or a first responder intentionally kills an unarmed black man, each person has to answer to the Lord. We who are left on this earth have to trust in the Lord as we get closer to standing before our maker. Our days on this earth are numbered, but where do you want to spend an eternity? You have to trust God to do what you cannot. It is easy to give your life, but it is difficult to allow the Lord to lead you into all truth. We must trust in the Lord with all our heart, lean not to our own understanding, and acknowledge him in all our ways because the heart is desperately wicked, who can know it.

We should avoid tantrums, murmuring, and mood swings. Be silent, submissive, and wait on the Lord. Wait, I say, on the Lord and he shall give you the ability to accomplish the desires of your heart. Here in lies the reason why

The Desires of Your Heart

Sunday school and Bible study is so important. People must be taught the word of God.

Sometimes we need to stop talking so negatively, realize the power of life and death lies in the tongue and close our mouths. Commit to the Lord whatever you do and your plans will succeed. If it is a home you want, higher education, marriage, or a greater work in the Lord, God wishes above all things that you would prosper and be in good health even as your soul prospers.

David preached to himself first and understood that he had to resist the devil. What is best practiced by others is that accepted by the person preaching it. We should never ask someone to do something that we will not do.

Spiritually, the desires of the heart should be lined up with all the cravings of the renewed sanctified soul and not the pleasure of flesh. It begs the question of what are the desires of the heart of a good man. The Bible exhorts one to know, love, and please God. Therefore, the desires of a

The Desires of Your Heart
good man are to make God his hope, be satisfied with His loving kindness, delight himself in the Lord and be obedient.

Chapter 3
What You Hope'n For

The race is not given to the swift or to the strong, but to the one that endures to the end. We don't have to wait until the battle is over, we can shout right now. It is important to understand that we cannot do anything we want, neglect God's work and expect to be blessed.

In his book entitled *White Coat Black Hat*, Carl Elliot, a professor of bioethics at the University of Minnesota explores the evolution and dark side of medicine. He became interested in the subject when a local psychiatrist asked if he could take his medical ethics class. Elliot naively stated yes and later found that the doctor was being disciplined by the state board of Minnesota for causing the death and injury of 46 people.[18]

If you are like me, you take or use to take a multivitamin everyday hoping that it would help increase your physical health. You exercise everyday hoping that it will help you live just a little bit longer. But studies like Professor Carl

What You Hope'n For

Elliott's can cause you to be scared of doctors. He talks about how there is no oversight of medicine, state boards' irresponsibleness, and how the pharmaceutical industry has really taken over medicine. He notes that medicine used to be morally policed from within, but since the pharmaceutical industry has taken over, that morality has decreased. According to Elliott, the pharmaceutical companies have an overwhelming influence over research studies, grant funding and the decisions doctors make regarding the care of their patients. This influence can lead to a continuation of drug trials even after patients have committed suicide.

For every one of you who puts their trust in a drug, you need to change the way you think. Elliot implies that drug testing should be taken out of the hands of the pharmacist because of the financial incentive to produce favorable findings with a limited number of tests.

What am I saying? We put our trust in a whole lot of stuff, but when it comes to putting our trust in the Lord, we

What You Hope'n For

worry about what other people think. We need to understand that Jesus is the reason we move, live and have our being and we should trust in him and not riches. This is the reason why Job asserts his freedom from trust in money, the rich young ruler went away sorrowfully, and it is easier for a camel to go through the eye of a needle, than for a rich man to enter into the kingdom of God. But, every one that puts God before brother, sister, father, mother, wife, or children for his sake shall receive a hundredfold, and shall inherit everlasting life.

Happy is the man that trusts God rather than money because his hope is in the Lord. Hope deferred maketh the heart sick, but when the desire cometh it causes happiness. It encompasses the mind, body and soul. Herein is the reason why the righteous man has hope when the wicked suffers death. As Abraham hoped against hope, had no grounds for hope, he was able to stagger not at the promises of God, exercise strong faith and be fully persuaded that God had his back. God would not have us be ignorant, even as others have no hope; we have the hope of the resurrection. This is the great antidote against the loss of loved ones. For if we have repented of our sin, committed our lives to the God, and we die, to be absent in the body is to be present with the Lord.

Hope is one of the three main elements of Christian character. It helps you get along well with others, be a team player and work hard on your job. Character is not just what you say, but what you live. When the scripture says seek ye first the kingdom of God and his righteousness, it is referring to seeking the character of Christ. Real hope can deliver the domestic violence victim in an abusive relationship, set the drug user and dealer free, take the taste of alcohol out of the mouth of the alcoholic, cause the prostitute to stop trick 'in and the pimp to stop pimp'in.

Like faith and love, hope can tell you who is a real Christian. Some people say they have the hope of Christ but they are always depressed, filled with lust and materialistic thinking. Rather than being a blessing to

What You Hope'n For

someone, their biggest concern is getting nails done, hair done and being fancy.

Paul tells us that we are joint heirs with Christ, are going to suffer some things, but with earnest expectation we wait for the revelation to come to pass. That creation is the way it is because of man, but both man and creation shall be delivered in the end. Man caused the curse so he has to share in the recovery. By one man did sin enter into the world and by one man can it be removed.

Hoping for the right things can be difficult without seeing what you're hoping for. But, we are saved with the help of hope, our salvation is hope, the expectation of that hope is the future, but it will soon be present.

Chapter 4
Heavenly Conversation

In her book entitled *Reclaiming Conversation, the Power of Talk in a Digital Age,* Sherry Turkle interviews several young college students over a period of time, and concludes that constant use of cell phones causes a lack of solitude, self-reflection, and empathy. Take for example Kristen who follows the Rule of Three and the Seven Minute Rule. She says texting is a commitment. When you text, you are promising your friends that you will be there for them. A text from a friend should be responded to within 5 minutes. She checks her phone periodically during class. If she gets a text from a friend that signals an emergency, she leaves class and goes to the bathroom to respond to the text. When asked what counts as an emergency she stated, "Boyfriend things. I'm the one that's stable, my friends need me." So, a few times a week this young economist walked out of her advanced seminar class to go to the bathroom, sit in the stall and text her friends.

Heavenly Conversation

Turkle argues when adults listen during a conversation they show children how to listen. When adults listen, children learn that it is comforting and pleasurable to be heard and understood. In addition, from listening, children learn how to negotiate, speak and listen with attention, control their emotions, problem solve, understand themselves and read other peoples' social cues.

Instead of promoting authenticity, social media encourages performance and allows you to put on your best face, says Turkle. For instance, according to Turkle, you post on Facebook what makes you look good. Thus a child does not become better at reading other people, but better at getting others to like them. When that child gets one hundred likes, they really get pumped up.

Turkle argues, with conversation comes the risk of vulnerability. Conversation exposes you to your shortcomings, inadequacies, and limitations. When we can see the other person's point of view, give into the needs of others, understand the feelings of others, and take the other

Heavenly Conversation

person's idea, perhaps you have had a great conversation. So many times we think if things are not done our way we have had a bad conversation, says Turkle.

Turkle points out that children are unhappy with how much attention parents give to their phones and desire to raise their children differently. Parents do not know how to have a conversation and are constantly on their phones, says one of Turkle's interviewees. A good conversation requires practice and confidence of expression. It is not necessary to always know the right answer, but it does require love and commitment to be around for the next conversation, according to Turkle.[43]

We struggle with putting our phones down. Kids spend an average of four point seven hours looking on their phones. As a result, it changes their body and brain. Looking down at your phone is equivalent of having an eight-year-old child sit on your neck. In some parts of Asia, eighty-ninety percent of the population is near sided. For all you Candy Crushers here is why it is difficult for you to put

Heavenly Conversation

your phone down. As you play the game, you achieve small goals that cause your brain to be rewarded with little bursts of dopamine. Eventually, you are rewarded with new content which gives you more dopamine. Together this creates what is called a compulsion loop. This happens to be the same loop that is responsible for the behaviors associated with nicotine and cocaine usage. So, all you Candy Crushers repent right now.

Young people use their phone to ward off boredom, have a fear of being without it, and as a result, their physical sleep is disrupted. The smart phone admits a blue light that alters our circadian rhythm which is linked to deep sleep. The smart phone screen admits a blue light that alters our circadian rhythms diminishing the time in deep sleep. The interruption of our circadian rhythm is also associated with diabetes, cancer, and obesity.

In her book *UnSelfie, Why Empathetic Kids Succeed in Our All about Me World*, Michele Borba found that a third of college students reported being so overwhelmed, it diminished their ability to function. She points out that more disturbing is the suicide rates of young girls. According to the Center of Disease Control, 150 girls between the ages of ten and fourteen committed suicide in 2014, a two hundred percent increase since 1999.[6]

Studies show that there is a correlation between our children's moral and mental health. The lack of right conduct, principles of rightness, and good ethical behavior is the driving force behind the stress, depression and anxiety children experience, including bullying and racist speech. This can be combated with the practice of empathy. In addition, being able to identify with thoughts and feelings can assist in lowering the aforementioned negative experiences.

This is where having a heavenly conversation with Jesus Christ comes into play. Once you have had a conversation with Jesus, you are equipped to minister the word of God to that person in need. When you have that heavenly conversation your daughter is less lightly to commit suicide, son feels good about himself, grandchild is no longer depressed, mother is encouraged and father is strengthened. A child alone with a problem has an emergency, but a child in a conversation with a grownup is facing a moment in life and learning how to handle it.

Our kids need to be more empathetic, less mean, happier and stronger mentally and emotionally. One girl in Turkle's book said she keeps no less than thirteen unread text on her phone. When asked about how it makes other's feel she seemed puzzled. Her response was she never really thought about their feelings.

In Turkle's book, a sixth grade student named Luis lost his father to suicide. He became fragile and dependent on his seventh grade sister Juanita. Anna, a friend of Juanita, got mad at Luis for interrupting her conversation with Juanita. Anna went on Facebook and posted, "I hope Luis ends up just like his father." The principle called Anna into the office and asked her why she did that. Anna's answer was it was just on Facebook. The principle was so mad he

Heavenly Conversation

became determined to make Anna cry before she left his office. He then had to call Anna's mom and explain why he made her cry, all because of the need to teach empathy. Anna believed that posting anything on Facebook was a license to harm and mistreat others.

People who would never allow them-selves to be bullies in person feel free to be a bully online. They are aggressive and vulgar on line but not in person. When you hear a voice and see a face, it reminds you of the person's humanity. Social media decreases self-control, civility and increases gratification, says Turkle. As soon as a person lays their phone on the table it disrupts the quality of conversation, Turkle proclaims. Heavenly conversation breeds empathy because it advocates face to face communication. Eye to eye contact can help increase our capacity to love and ability to process another's feelings and intentions. Kids who can collaborate, innovate and problem solve are much happier. Fathers need heavenly conversation to teach their children how to work and cooperate with others. Are you teaching your child how to collaborate or is it all about your child? Many adults are not team players, thus it is difficult for them to teach their child this principle.

Jesus taught that a good leader is a good follower, we should submit to one another and if anyone is caught in a transgression, you who are spiritual restore such a one. Furthermore, he that is greatest among us, let him serve. When Jesus told the disciples he was coming back, the disciples believing he had positions to give out were more concerned about office and rank. Jesus was about to die and all the disciples could think about is where their office would be. They had a love for power, which shows selfishness can find its way in secret places of the church.

For a heavenly conversation look no further than Jesus' talk with Nicodemus. We learn that the conversation may not go the way you think it should. Jesus didn't beat around the bush with him. He bluntly told Nicodemus, if you are not born again you will not see me in the end. Though the conversation may not have gone the way

Heavenly Conversation

Nicodemus thought, it was heavenly. It was heavenly because Nicodemus was tough and able to take it; he was not extolled by Jesus, given a plaque for his compliments, and he does not go away sorrowful like the rich young ruler. You can tell Nicodemus gets it because he asks Jesus how he could attain salvation and Jesus was able to move on and communicate truth.

You have had a heavenly conversation when you do what God tells you to do. When you are a witness for Jesus, show love to your brother, take care of your children, and lend a helping hand to the stranger, the world will know you have had a heavenly conversation with the Lord. But when we sin, we don't want to have a conversation with God. Contrary to popular belief, this is when we need it the most. Adam was afraid to have a conversation with God because he had sinned.

Paul tells the disciples to have a heavenly conversation, rejoice in the Lord and beware of evil doers. He encourages them to have no confidence in thinking they can do anything without the help of others. Paul further implied that he was not condemning them because he realized he had persecuted the church. He commanded the disciples to know Jesus in the power of his resurrection, not be an enemy of God or mind earthly things.

Our citizenship and life should not be in earthly treasure, but heavenly citizenship has its existence in heaven. So, you should focus on Jesus who makes intercession for you. He is the giver of life. Therefore, we should look to the hills from which cometh our help, for our help comes from the Lord. Just as the coffee house historically has been the place to learn, have freedom of thought, courage and difficult conversation, so too is the church the place for the Christian to learn, have spiritual freedom, gain righteous courage and have heavenly conversation.

Chapter 5
Building Bridges with Love

Charles Spurgeon, a very influential British Baptist Preacher in the 1800's stated, "I hold very stern opinions with regard to Christian men who have fallen into gross sin. I rejoice that they may be truly converted, and may be with caution received into the church, but I gravely question whether a man who has grossly sinned should be very readily restored to the pulpit. When a preacher of righteousness has stood in the way of sinners, he should never again open his lips in the great congregation until his repentance is as great as his sin. My belief is that we should be very slow to help back to the pulpit men who have been tried and proved themselves unable to stand the crucial tests of ministerial life." [16]

Spurgeon pastored the New Park Street Chapel in London for 38 years, preached to over ten million people in his life time, preached up to ten times per week, and his sermons were translated into many languages. He started a college, arguably has more material in print than anybody, and was known as the prince of preachers. He did not believe once a person was saved he was always saved, but believed sin separated man from God. He further believed that man always had an advocate with the Father and could be restored to preaching because God is a loving father. He believed that even the darkest person could be redeemed and had value.

There are many people who start their day with no purpose. If you realize that you've been blessed, you should always desire to be a blessing to someone else. The blessed believe, great is the Lord and he's greatly to be praised. The holy person begins his day with the understanding it is the day that the Lord has made and he should be glad in it. God's people daily enter into his gates with thanksgiving and into his courts with praise, knowing it is impossible to go under for going over, because greater is he that is in them than he that is in the world.

Timothy said supplications, prayers, intercessions, and giving of thanks should be made for all men, even your enemies. He admonishes us to lead a quiet and peaceable life in all godliness and honesty and do what is good and acceptable in the sight of God. So, my prayer is that you are not deceived because God is not mocked and whatsoever a man seweth that shall he also reap. My hope is that the Lord brings us all to the place where we are more loving toward each other and when we speak our words are always seasoned with grace. Jesus said it is easy to love those that love you, but the real challenge is to love that man, woman, boy or girl who we consider to be unlovable.

During troubled times I always try to remember to consult God because for every natural situation there is a spiritual answer. The word of God is sharper than any two edged sword, the grass withereth, the flower fadeth, but the word of God is going to last forever. Heaven and earth will pass way, but the word of God is going to last throughout eternity.

If you are like me, you are exhausted from seeing us mistreat each other. No race, creed or color can claim an exemption in the area of hate. I've observed black people mistreat white people, white people mistreat black people, and both races mistreat people of their own race. I've even observed presidential contenders mistreat people of Middle Eastern descent.

The people of God foresaw their freedom drawing near and began to blaspheme the name of the Lord by speaking evil against dignitaries. What God wanted his people to understand and what Paul was trying to teach Timothy, a young pastor, was he so loved the world that he gave his only begotten son. Jesus is a redeemer and we are bought with a price. Therefore, he who is without sin cast the first stone.

The Second Epistle of Peter states that God is not slack concerning his promise, not willing that any should perish and that all would come to repentance. I certainly am glad

Building Bridges with Love

that God is merciful, kind and long suffering because I know if it were not for the Lord I would have been grave yard dead a long time ago. From being a fornicator to smoking wack, you name it I did it before accepting Christ. Only Satan could drive a person to smoke a marijuana cigarette dipped in a liquid substance used as an elephant tranquilizer. I am so glad that who the Son sets free is free indeed.

One of the biggest questions facing Americans today is what will make us safe. I along with members of my church sincerely prayed for President George Bush every week at Wednesday night prayer while he was in office. What would you have done after 9-11? It didn't matter to me that he was a Republican president and I am a Democrat, and I'm sure that many Republicans have prayed for President Obama. But, we should never use race to divide people. We should always be willing to build people up and give constructive criticism. While we should always be a builder, to the contrary, there were people who prayed for President Bush, but not for

Building Bridges with Love

President Obama, just because of the color of his skin. This was done even though during his administration no one was water boarded. When has it ever been okay to torture somebody? President Bush and President Obama promoted love, respect and kindness for all mankind. My point is we ought to always pray for leaders. Secretary Hillary Clinton is right, love will make us safer.

Romans thirteen says let every soul be subject unto the higher powers. For there is no power but of God, and the powers that be are ordained of God. Whosoever therefore resisteth the power resisteth the ordinance of God and they that resist shall receive to themselves damnation. Rulers are not the terror to good work and are the ministers of God to thee for good. Regarding dignitaries, Romans thirteen instructs us how to govern ourselves. Christians are supposed to be the salt of the earth, light of the world, and should never fight with police or curse judges. Therefore, you cannot be a follower of Christ and not subject yourself to the laws of the land.

Building Bridges with Love

Though we have inalienable rights and it is okay to make a complaint, we cannot take the law into our own hands. There is often conflict between the moral and the social, but Christians are charged with redressing the social through the spiritual. We have the right to protest, but should always disapprove of inordinate behavior toward the magistrates. The sinner may act a fool, but not Christians.

Having lived in a metropolitan area that has a population of over a hundred and fifty thousand people, it is disappointing that McLean County, Illinois, in 2016 still has never had a person of color sit on the bench. This is especially disturbing because a high percentage of African Americans are processed through the court system in this county. When I asked a chief judge what his thoughts were about the possibility of appointing a judge of color, his response was the person has to have practiced law. I have worked as a probation officer for thirty years, taught criminology at Heartland Community College for twenty years, and studied the criminal justice system for thirty-five years. I've known for a long time that in order to become a judge one first has to be a practicing attorney. It is my hope that one day the court will have the courage to appoint a person of color to the bench in the Eleventh Judicial Circuit in the state of Illinois.

It is okay to make a complaint, but we cannot put a gun to someone's head in an attempt to make them change. We teach our children the importance of moral integrity, so how much the more should adults do the right thing. The word of God says be ye angry and sin not. Be mad at the devil because we wrestle not against flesh and blood but against principalities in high places. When you make a complaint be calm, cool and collected. When the Bible says seek ye first the kingdom of God and his righteousness, it is instructing us to take on the character of Christ. Therefore, you are guaranteed to successfully govern yourself in a righteous and lawful manner. We should love people, and never be evil, vengeful and vindictive. The Uniform Crime Report is evidence of people not putting on the whole armor of God and their anger driving them to commit criminal behavior.

Here too lies the reason why we have such poor race relations. It is this same disregard for all men that causes us to have bad race relations. We have to care enough about other races of people if we want to make a difference. I'm convinced that if we would see things through the eyes of God, good race relations are guaranteed. Though they may not always govern themselves by the word of God, I'm glad I taught my children, Dewhitt and Whitney, to love all humanity.

Chapter 6
The Law of Reciprocity

How does the law of reciprocity apply to us as a church? How should we use it in our activities and business? How does it apply to our families? Should we use it and what results should we expect?

Give and it shall be given unto you in good measure, press down, shaken together and running over shall men give into your bosom. God so loved the world that he gave his only begotten son. When he gave he gave his best. While we were yet sinners Christ died for us. Contrary to many who have a self-righteous belief, did you know that true love is giving and expecting something in return? You may be saying to yourself, I can give and it is not necessary that I receive anything in return. Stop lying!

Though this is the dispensation of grace, we live in a capitalistic society and need to understand that nothing is free. No one should expect to be loved without giving love or receive and never give anything in return. Ask

The Law of Reciprocity

yourself how you would feel if in a relationship you were constantly giving and it was not being reciprocated. You did everything in your power to help someone and once the person experienced success, they forgot all about you. It goes without saying the person is selfish, self-centered and egotistical, but you would feel rejected. I don't know about you, but I hate rejection.

I'm convinced that it is difficult for people to love because they lack understanding on how to love and the benefits of loving someone. Once a person knows how to love and the benefits of love, that knowledge can be applied and the person will be blessed.

Ask any man who pays the bills, does all the domestic duties which includes attending to all the needs of his children, and his wife constantly spends, and is responsible for nothing and he will tell you that is a marriage from hell. Ask any woman whose husband is a failure at being prophet, priest and king in the home, mismanages the finances, and sits on his butt and she too will say it is a marriage from hell.

God did not intend for it to be as aforementioned. When he gave his life to redeem us, he was expecting something in return. God is love. Therefore, if men would love others like God loves them, there would be a decrease in mistreatment, infidelity and even murder. It is impossible to love God and mistreat others if you truly love God as his word says that you should. For if you say you love God whom you have never seen and hate your brother who you see every day, you are a liar, and cannot be considered as one who loves God. We show love for our jobs, businesses, and material possessions, but once we get what we want, we forget all about God and the people who helped us accomplish our goal. This is not God and it is not right.

When Jesus gave his sermon on the mount, he informed the disciples that his time was almost up and he was going to be leaving them. At that time, he advised his people to

The Law of Reciprocity

harbor not the love he gave them. He wanted the disciples to know that he rains on the just and unjust. He does this because he desires that the righteous would remain and the unrighteous would be converted. Reciprocity is always at work, it is a mutual or cooperative interchange of favors or privileges, a spiritual law that is immutable, unbreakable and universal.

Blessed are the merciful, for they will be shown mercy, we receive what we give away. The golden rule says do to others as you would have them do to you. Seek first the kingdom of God and his righteousness and all these things shall be added unto you. If we give God what he asks for, righteousness, sensitivity to his will, kingdom work, he in turn provides us things we need. Thus, this is the reason the Psalmist says I was young and now I am old, yet I have never seen the righteous forsaken or his seed begging bread.

God's provision for his people is part of a covenant he has made with us and it is based on reciprocity. Bring the

The Law of Reciprocity

whole tithe into the storehouse that there may be food in my house. Test me and see if I will not pour you out a blessing that you will not have room enough to receive. This shows that reciprocity applies to finances, but you can never out give God. I'm in the red, white and the blue when it comes to owing him because I realize you cannot out give God. You give in relation to your ability and he gives in relation to his ability.

The person who sows to please God will reap a harvest at the proper time, and ultimately gain eternal life. Though we receive in proportion to our giving, it does not mean we should have a mercenary approach to giving-if I give then I'll get. We should not serve God or each other just for what we can get out of it.

The rich young man came to Jesus and asked how to inherit eternal life. Jesus answered, if you want to be perfect, go sell your possessions and give to the poor, and you will have treasure in heaven. When the young man heard this, he went away sad, because he had great wealth.

The Law of Reciprocity

Then Jesus said to his disciples, I tell you the truth, it is hard for a rich man to enter the kingdom of heaven. Again I tell you, it is easier for a camel to go through the eye of a needle than for a rich man to enter the kingdom of God.

Jesus was not saying that you will not go to heaven or experience the kingdom of God if you have a large bank account. If you are a typical rich person, your money is very important to you, but you have to be careful that it does not become your god. You spiritually own nothing and must consider everything you have as nothing compared to Jesus. You must be prepared to leave everything behind as if it were trash. We do not make investments in God's kingdom. We give gifts and offerings, give up ownership and believe what you give away is no longer yours.

We could apply the law of reciprocity and claim that we should only experience good. However, has anyone ever told you that if you do God's work you will experience difficulty, financial need or social pressure? Paul was

The Law of Reciprocity

beaten publicly by a mob, severely flogged, homeless, and brutally mistreated. Didn't Paul have enough faith? Didn't he use the principles of the kingdom? Or is it just our inclination to look at the kingdom as a way to benefit? As believers, we anticipate good things from God to show his desire for us to prosper and have material blessings, but things are not always good.

The New Testament covenant is different from the Old Testament covenant. The Old Testament contained material covenants, emphasized material well being, prosperity, and right actions. The New Testament covenant is original and better because it emphasizes spiritual growth, a right relationship with God, righteous attitudes, and involvement in God's kingdom.

Be very careful about applying old covenant material promises to New Testament experience. Materialism is completely out of place in the New Testament. Are you willing to renounce all your possessions, finances, family & friends? Are you willing, starting today, to live in poverty, to be abused and despised because you're a Christian? If that's what it would mean for you to serve God, would you be willing to do it? Jesus said that if you put your hand to the plow and look back, you're not worthy to follow him. He further said remember Lot's wife; she hesitated long enough to take one last look at her old life, her home and friends, and it cost her life. Decide now who you will serve. Serving Christ means you will renounce everything else. The Law of Reciprocity is very real. The one who sows to please his sinful nature, from that nature will reap destruction, but the one who sows to please the Spirit, from the Spirit will reap eternal life.

Chapter 7
Take Fast Hold of Instructions

Wisdom is a great principle that we all should seek after and prescribing to it will bring us honor, peace and joy. God's wisdom leads us into the right paths, teaches us how to season our words with grace, and gives us long life if we take fast hold of it. Taking fast hold of instructions teaches us how to follow, means good followers become good leaders, and instructs us that we do not always have to be out front. Being in a position to support someone's idea can bring pleasure to the soul. Many people struggle to love the person who thinks he knows it all. This is the type of person who never makes a mistake, whose suggestion is always the best proposal, and who does not understand that all people are important and every issue counts.

Following directions is a fundamental skill taught to us from an early age. While it may seem logical and even straightforward to follow directions, failure to do so could be harmful or even fatal. One of the most notable fugitive

Take Fast Hold of Instructions

slaves of American history and conductors of the Underground Railroad was Harriet Tubman. Born into slavery, Tubman escaped from her master's plantation in 1849. Between 1850 and 1860, she returned to the South numerous times to help other slaves to freedom, guiding them through the lands she knew well. She alone aided an estimated 300 people to escape from slavery, including her parents. During this time, there was a $40,000 bounty for her, payable to anyone who could capture her and bring her back to slavery. If you were a runaway slave under her guidance, you could lose your life if you did not follow her instructions.[13]

Tubman, born a slave, was hired, leased or rented out for a price by her master as a nursemaid. Not only was her master making money off her as a slave, but as a nursemaid as well. For those of you who do not know what a nursemaid was, a nursemaid watched young children. Tubman was charged with watching the children of slave owners. She had to make sure the child did not cry at night. If the child cried, she could be whipped by

Take Fast Hold of Instructions

the baby's mother. Slavery was a mental, emotional, spiritual and physical death sentence, and drove Tubman to follow the North Star to escape at the first opportunity. Most of us would not have lasted a day in slavery. Just as Tubman, I too would have tried to escape. You would have had to kill me to remain in such inhumane conditions.

Using my Holy Ghost imagination, I can see some of the saints of the highest God, you know the ones who think they know it all, saying to Tubman, no it's not that way it's this way. For those of you looking for a caboose, it was not a traditional railroad. If you have visited the Underground Railroad in Cincinnati, Ohio you know that it was a critical or decisive system of transportation. What do I mean decisive? Tubman had to be able to make choices quickly with confidence and those decisions had to be clear and obvious. She could not stand there and look around, asking which way should I go? She was so skillful that she never got caught. She was the conductor and instrumentalist. Tubman had to know where the secret network of safe houses were, Jerseyville, Galesburg and

Jacksonville, Illinois were three of the fifty safe houses. Runaway slaves stayed at these safe houses on their journey north to freedom.

Some people could not follow you across the street even if you lead them by the hand. Have you ever met one of those people who you cannot tell anything because they know it all and have an opinion on everything no matter what the subject? They are opinionated, bombastic, terrible listeners and rarely admit to not having enough knowledge to give an opinion because humility is not in their blood. This person stays set on transmit and not receive. They want to be the one who transmits their pearls of wisdom, what they do not know is not worth knowing, and when they do learn something, according to them, they knew it already. These people are smart, but their belief that they know it all makes them narrow minded and less able to learn.

Many people lack good active listening skills that prevent them from taking fast hold of instructions. To be a good active listener you have to look at the person who is talking, think about what is being said, wait your turn to talk and then say what you want to say. The know it all often puts you down without meaning to, knows everything and you know nothing, damages your self-esteem, and anything you know is because of them. They say things like, if I offended you I am sorry and if I said something wrong I apologize. This is the response you get after they have roasted you so bad that you are burnt up and smell like smoke. This is a form of greed in the sense that they want to be the director all the time. It is like grabbing all the food at the dinner table, something growing up you did not do in my house if you wanted to live to see tomorrow.

For an example of a know it all look no further than the Sadducees and Pharisees. While the Pharisees believed in angels and the afterlife, they believed in the written and oral law. The Sadducees blatantly denied the resurrection and the spirit world. Both sects had flaws, but you couldn't tell them anything.

Solomon, one of the wisest men ever, persuades us to be obedient. He proclaims we should take fast hold of instructions because temptation is forever present and the liability of falling into temptation is great. Solomon implies to lack the desire for accountability, responsibility and dependability causes damage, injury and harm to others. Instructions he declared is synonymous with wisdom.

God's wisdom is to be held on to like a shipwrecked sinking sailor because it is the bestowal of life. Through wisdom we experience order to our chaos, and it prevents us from lying, cheating and stealing. You should want it more than your necessary food. It does have a prerequisite and that is salvation. You cannot have wisdom without it. The Bible declares, the fear of the Lord is the beginning of wisdom and you cannot say you fear the Lord if you do not allow him to lord over you. Accepting Christ is permitting wisdom to govern your thoughts, feelings, attitudes and beliefs. In return you are victorious over all your circumstances.

Worldly wisdom is something we all are born with. This type of wisdom is a way that seems right to a man, but the end thereof is the way of death. A soul without true wisdom is a dead soul. Without it you are subject to be contemptible, wretched, disgraceful and dishonorable. You can have all the money in the world and still die without an understanding. So think it not strange that people die without God or the hope of Christ. Life depends upon observance of the precepts of wisdom. When you have wisdom life is secured, when you lose wisdom, life becomes hopeless. Wisdom is not the law, but is the doctrine of Jesus Christ, mind and will of God concerning salvation of men, grace of God, and doctrine of peace, pardon, righteousness and eternal life.

How do we know if we have taken hold of instructions? It is not just head knowledge or a form of Godliness. It is received in the heart which means it is mixed with faith

Take Fast Hold of Instructions

when heard. Faith comes by hearing, hearing by the word of God. Faith is the substance of things hoped for and evidence of things not seen. Couple that with the fact that James said faith without works is dead and you are taking fast hold of instructions. Once it is received in the heart you begin to practice it and become a doer. So, taking fast hold of instructions means you are a practitioner of righteousness, doer, and your works prove you are a workman or workwoman.

How long should you hold on to it? Herein is the problem that most of us have, holding on to wisdom. How does wisdom get taken? First, you cannot hold on to it if you never get it, so having it is a good thing. Second, we let it go. We drop it, depart from it, neglect it and are careless with it. Finally, it can be taken by force and fraud, and Satan is always the root cause.

How can we keep from dropping it? We should guard it by keeping our eyes on Jesus Christ himself. He is the way, the truth and the life, no man comes to the father

Take Fast Hold of Instructions accept through Christ as he is the author and maintainer of our spiritual life. Proverbs suggest what is needed is earnest effort. If you are giving earnest effort you do not lead silly women laden with sin captive, give into lustful desires, nor proceed in the way that is wrong, but you always strive to do what is right.

Chapter 8

Joy Cometh in the Morning

"I will extol thee O LORD for thou hast lifted me up, and hast not made my foes to rejoice over me. O LORD my God, I cried unto thee, and thou hast healed me. O LORD, thou hast brought up my soul from the grave. Thou hast kept me alive, that I should not go down to the pit. Sing unto the LORD, O ye saints of his, and give thanks at the remembrance of his holiness. For his anger endureth but a moment, in his favor is life, weeping may endure for a night, but joy cometh in the morning" (Psalm 30:1-5 KJV).

It is always good to be in the house of the Lord. David said I was glad when they said unto me let us go into the house of the Lord. He knew that in the house of the Lord he could find strength, fellowship, peace and joy. I am sure you know the life of David. Though he was a man after God's own heart, he impregnated Bathsheba, put her husband Uriah on the front line of a war which resulted in Uriah's death, but who certainly is present with the Lord. Having been an accessory to murder, it is unquestionably

Joy Cometh in the Morning

why David praised the Lord so much. To those who believe you can never be redeemed, let this be an example to you of God's saving power. I can hear David saying to whom much is given much is required, all things work together for good to those who love the Lord and are called according to his purpose, trust in the Lord with all your heart and lean not to your own understanding, weeping may endure for a night, but joy cometh in the morning.

There is something to be said about the grace of God. Grace can be defined as loveliness, style and beauty, but in Godly terms it is unwarranted, unearned and undeserved favor. Favor can be defined as an act of kindness or a good deed. Together you have unwarranted kindness, unearned goodness and undeserved compassion. You may be wondering what grace has to do with joy. The Greek words for joy and grace are related and it is grace that causes joy. Thus, you cannot have joy without grace.

Joy Cometh in the Morning

The book of James says whence come wars and fighting. James was dealing with people who called themselves Christians, but were fighting each other. Christians fight one another because of what is within them, James proclaims. He points out that evil, unethical and mean spirited behavior many times is simply the result of what is already in the person, and informs us that not even Satan is the blame. James said let no man say when he is tempted, I am tempted of God; for God cannot be tempted with evil, neither tempt he any man. But every man is tempted, when he is drawn away of his own lust and enticed. So, whether it is fighting each other, committing a sexual sin or murder, James teaches that it originates from within and we can be our own worst enemy.

To those who pray, war not, and show forth love, God promises his blessings. He is not so interested in those who pray for pleasures, are pride filled, and pray amiss. These individuals are people who do not submit to doing things the right way, fail to resist wrong and run to trouble rather than away. Instead of being drawn to that which is

Joy Cometh in the Morning

right, they are drawn to mistreatment, oppression, and domination. This in turn opens the person up to being afflicted, having their laughter be turned to mourning, and their joy to heaviness.

You can have joy if you really want it, but it is conditional and provisional. Joy is a byproduct, side effect, result or consequence of obedience. You cannot mistreat, abuse, and cause harm to others, and have joy because God expects you to live peaceable among all men. You cannot engage in fornication, adultery or premarital sex without the risk of being infected with HIV or any sexual transmitted disease which certainly would not bring you joy. So, if joy is a byproduct of obedience, it cannot be a derivative of disobedience. For many, here in is the reason why joy is elusive and hopelessness is always at their doorstep.

There is a difference between our joy and God's joy. Many may believe they have the joy of the Lord due to earthly possessions such as money, a nice car, extravagant

Joy Cometh in the Morning

home, but that is not necessary to have the joy of the Lord. God's joy is synonymous with heaven, service to God and faithfulness. If you are faithful over the small things, you then qualify yourself to be a ruler over many things with access to the Lord's joy.

How do we keep joy? Your joy will be sustained by abiding in the love of God. You abide in the love of God by keeping his commandments. As a result, Jesus himself received joy. This is also evidenced by David in his recovery from a dangerous sickness from which God delivered him. Upon his recovery from the illness, David praises God for healing, calls on others to praise him, recalls his complaints, demonstrates thankfulness and implies that you too should do the same.

Paul and Silas, servants of God who were telling men how to be saved, cast an evil spirit out of a female slave who earned a great deal of money for her master. When her owners realized that their hope of making money was gone, Paul and Silas were seized and dragged into the

Joy Cometh in the Morning

marketplace to face the authorities. They were brought before the magistrates who ordered them to be stripped and beaten with rods. After being flogged, they were thrown into prison, and the jailer was commanded to guard them carefully. The jailer put them in the inner cell and fastened their feet in the stocks. About midnight Paul and Silas prayed and began to sing hymns to God. All at once the prison doors flew open, everyone's chains came loose, and the jailer, rather than take his own life accepted Christ.

If you are like me you have received the joy of the Lord. Just when I thought I was at my wits end with no way of escape, God stepped into my life. All because I took stock in looking to the hills from which cometh my help and realized my help came from the Lord. David reminds us to never forget how God has and can deliver anyone from alcohol, drugs, fornication, prostitution, and all the devices of the enemy. Though things may seem bad at times, never forget how far God has brought you. If he is able to deliver you, he is well able to keep you from falling, but should you fall you have an advocate with the Father.

Joy Cometh in the Morning

Absalom, the son of David, noted for his personal beauty had an evil desire to supplant his own father and committed fratricide. Despite the homicidal desires toward him by his own son, David called on others to praise the Lord because he understood God had been good to him. Has God been good to you? If he has, you should always praise him with the fruit of your lips, and with the raising and clapping of your hands. This gives God a vote of confidence and you can rest assured that joy is on the way.

Chapter 9
Be a Giver and Not a Taker

"Judge not, and ye shall not be judged, condemn not, and ye shall not be condemned, forgive, and ye shall be forgiven, give and it shall be given unto you, good measure, pressed down, and shaken together, and running over, shall men give into your bosom. For with the same measure that ye mete withal it shall be measured to you again. And he spoke a parable unto them; can the blind lead the blind? Shall they not both fall into the ditch? The disciple is not above his master, but every one that is perfect shall be as his master. And why behold thou the mote that is in thy brother's eye, but perceive not the beam that is in thine own eye? Either how can thou say to thy brother, brother, let me pull out the mote that is in thine eye, when thou thyself beholdest not the beam that is in thine own eye? Thou hypocrite, cast out first the beam out of thine own eye, and then shalt thou see clearly to pull out the mote that is in thy brother's eye" (Luke 6:37-42).

Be a Giver Not a Taker

A mother wanted to teach her daughter a moral lesson. She gave the little girl a quarter and a dollar for church, "Put whichever one you want in the collection plate and keep the other for yourself," she told the girl. When they were coming out of church, the mother asked her daughter which amount she had given.

"Well," said the little girl, "I was going to give the dollar, but just before the collection the man in the pulpit said that we should all be cheerful givers. I knew I'd be a lot more cheerful if I gave the quarter, so I did."[12] Be a giver and not a taker.

I recently attended my alma mater, Lincoln University, for homecoming and observed at halftime of the football game there was an acknowledgement of those who made significant financial contributions to the school. Giant mock sized checks were paraded to thank and acknowledge alumni for giving, encourage more alumni to give and contribute to LU, including my daughter who will soon be an alumnus, and inspire the Blue Tiger faithful to

Be a Giver Not a Taker

help financially strengthen the school. Be a giver and not a taker.

As a Probation Officer, I've taken breakfast to the home of juvenile offenders hoping to encourage them to attend school on a regular basis. I too have taken them to ballgames with hope that they would demonstrate socially appropriate behavior, and taught them how to set goals while facilitating Moral Reconation Therapy, a cognitive based program designed to lower offender recidivism.

As a college professor I do my best to teach students the importance of giving back to the community. Many of my students, who are now public servants, serve on community boards, and some are my colleagues at the McLean County Probation Department. There is no greater joy than knowing you played a role in helping a student accomplish a goal. In addition, I purchased the first McLean County Youthbuild home and have served on the Board since its inception. Be a giver and not a taker.

Be a Giver Not a Taker

To illustrate that you can be a taker and not a giver as a public servant, look no further than Kwame Kilpatrick who was elected Mayor of Detroit. After being elected, he betrayed the trust of the people, became engaged in an extra marital affair with his chief of staff, Christine Beatty, resulting in one of the biggest scandals in Detroit history. Beatty in *Essence Magazine* reported that for years she would think fondly of her and Mr. Kilpatrick's first kiss shared sitting on his mother's couch. She further reported that the kiss was passionate yet gentle, the sweetest thing she had ever experienced. Can you imagine how it felt to be Mrs. Kilpatrick and Mr. Beatty?

Mrs. Beatty reported that she and Mr. Kilpatrick would find any spare time they could to be together, at the office or at her home when her children were not there. She further reported that Mr. Kilpatrick made her laugh, angry, propelled her to ecstasy, reduced her to tears, but most important, she felt he loved her unconditionally. She testified how she let her family down, got kicked out of

Be a Giver Not a Taker

law school, disgraced her family and friends and let her city down.

Mr. Kilpatrick's selfish and greedy motives drove him to use civic funds as his personal piggy bank, lie on the stand in a court of law, and many believe made him conspire to have Tamara Green murdered. He was eventually forced to resign, moved to Texas and took a six figure job. He refused to pay restitution to the city of Detroit, argued he could only pay sixteen dollars per month, yet he was living in a gated community, paying $2,600.00 a month mortgage, all while driving a Cadillac Escalade. In addition, Kilpatrick caused his mother to lose her state senate seat she held for seven years, allowed his father and school friends to fix contracts and get kickbacks from taxpayer money. Instead of resigning his position and receiving a minor sentence, Kilpatrick got charged with bribery, fraud, tax evasion, and racketeering, forcing him to resign. I'm convinced he thought he was Al Capone. He is now serving a 28-year federal prison sentence. Be a giver and not a taker.[4]

Be a Giver Not a Taker

You might be thinking to yourself that would never happen in the church. Racketeering laws have been used against pro-lifers for blocking abortion clinics, priests of the Catholic Church for allowing children to be molested, and Edward Mackenzie Jr., an admitted enforcer and member of the Boston Society of the New Jerusalem Church for racketeering, mail fraud and money laundering. He cost that church millions of dollars and looted their assets. Be a giver not a taker.

Being a taker and not a giver can catapult you from touchdown to lockdown. To illustrate my point, look no further than Sam Hurd and Daryl Hanley. Hanley went to UCLA, was drafted in the second round by the St. Louis Rams, signed a 1.5 million-dollar contract, was rookie of the year and was about to sign an eight-million-dollar contract. He ran into an old friend who propositioned him to deal drugs. Hanley and his associate used a nineteen-year-old cheerleader to assist in their racket. Hanley is currently serving a forty-one-year federal prison sentence. The young cheerleader who involved herself simply

Be a Giver Not a Taker

because she wanted to date Hanley, ended up with a federal record and served four months in federal prison. After being sentenced to prison, Hanley attempted to deal drugs from prison, threatened a judge, and put a hit out on the nineteen-year-old cheerleader. He recently changed his life, but the damage has been done. All this after being raised right by his parents, be a giver not a taker.

Sam Hurd, a young man who attended Northern Illinois University, did not get drafted, but earned a tryout with America's team, the Dallas Cowboys. A wide receiver that had a gift of going up and getting the ball over defenders, had twenty-one touch downs in four years at NIU and was kept out of trouble by his family, and saved eighty-eight thousand dollars to purchase a home for his parents. He was on the verge of signing a 4.1-million-dollar contract with the Chicago Bears until he was indicted on the charge of conspiracy with intent to deliver and was sentenced to fifteen years in prison. For Hurd and Hanley it all began with wanting to have more money.

Be a Giver Not a Taker

The love of money is the root of all evil, be a giver not a taker.[10]

Giving comes in many different forms, and is a form of Godly worship. You can be a public servant and give back by serving others as a school teacher, nurse, trash collector, or insurance agent. You can support underprivileged children by donating to the Boys and Girls Club, being an advocate for Big Brother Big Sisters, and giving to the Center for Youth and Family Solutions. Serving on the board of a non for profit organization, volunteering to cut the grass of an elderly person and washing a widow's windows are all ways to serve your community. Christian people ought to be making contributions to God, family, church, neighborhoods, and schools. Always try to live your life based on these words, give and it shall be given unto you, in good measure, press down shaken together and running over shall men give to you, it is better to give than to receive, and be a giver not a taker.

Chapter 10
For the Love of Money

"If any man teach otherwise, and consent not to wholesome words, even the words of our Lord Jesus Christ, and to the doctrine which is according to godliness; he is proud, knowing nothing, but doting about questions and strife of words, whereof cometh envy, strife, railings, evil surmising, perverse disputing of men of corrupt minds, and destitute of the truth, supposing that gain is godliness: from such withdraw thyself. But godliness with contentment is great gain. For we brought nothing into this world and it is certain we can carry nothing out. Having food and raiment let us be therewith content, but they that will be rich fall into temptation and a snare, and into many foolish and hurtful lusts, which drown men in destruction and perdition. For the love of money is the root of all evil: which while some coveted after, they have erred from the faith, and pierced themselves through with many sorrows. But thou, O man of God, flee these things; and follow after righteousness, godliness, faith, love, patience, meekness" (I Timothy 6:3-11).

For the Love of Money

In a CNN interview of the great Ervin Magic Johnson, Magic in response to Donald Sterling states, "I'm not going to sit here and let Donald Sterling disrupt my day, my year, and my month. I'm one of the most honest guys you're ever going to talk to. I don't steal, I don't set people up, and I don't do those types of things. I don't know that young lady. I took a picture and all of a sudden I'm in the middle of this mess. But, at the same time I will not let you attack me without responding. You don't want me to come to your games? I won't come. But you don't want blacks to come? I'm going to fight for those people because I'm a proud black man. I'm one of the leaders in the black community and I take that role seriously." Magic further reminded Donald Sterling that he has sent more than ten thousand minorities to college via the Magic Johnson Foundation and has invested millions of dollars in urban cities and businesses.[2]

When you make accusations against somebody, you had better do your homework, research, and have documentation to back it up. Magic Johnson does not

For the Love of Money

have AIDS, he has HIV. He's not an employee of a business, he OWNS the LA Dodgers. Wealthy African Americans do help the black community. Spike Lee, Tyler Perry, Oprah Winfred, Michael Jordan and many more give back to the black community. So, Mr. Sterling's accusation is a lie straight from the pit of hell.

Paul warns Timothy that piety can be used as a means of gain and one can be pious and still be discontented with their present possessions. Paul further implies that piety can be used as a cloak of covetousness. Meaning, it can be used as a disguise, cover up, camouflage to conceal an underlying motive. In other words, piety can be used for greed. By implying that Jews give back to their communities and African Americans do not, this is an attempt to turn Jews against the black community, and is divisive, all for the love of money. One thing I cannot stand is a phony person masquerading around, full of pride, with a haughty spirit engaging in evil guessing, wicked assumptions and immoral conclusions without giving people the benefit of the doubt.

For the Love of Money

For those of you, who think gain is success, think again. Paul could not have made it clearer, gain is not necessarily godliness. Just because you are monetarily wealthy does not mean you are a Christian or successful from a spiritual perspective. So, when Donald Sterling asks the question, what hospital Magic Johnson gives to, he thinks he has cornered the market on righteousness because he is wealthy and capable of giving to charity. Paul instructs Christian people to withdraw themselves from pride filled individuals such as Mr. Sterling. Withdraw, but pray for him. So, Magic was right when he said that he would continue to speak to Mr. Sterling and pray for him. Magic understands that the love of money is the root of all evil.

For African Americans giving back to the black community look no further than Madam CJ Walker. Born Sarah Breedlove on a cotton plantation in Louisiana, Breedlove was the first African American female millionaire. Orphaned at age seven, widowed with a two-year-old daughter, she moved to St. Louis where on a laundress salary, she educated her daughter and sent her to

For the Love of Money

Knoxville College, a Historical Black College. She started her own line of hair care products that grew to include a beauty school in Pittsburgh, Indianapolis and Harlem. By 1916 her company included twenty thousand agents, both men and women, in the United States, Central America, and the Caribbean. She was a well known philanthropist, gave to the black community, and was a strong advocate for black women's economic independence when the only other option at the time was domestic work and sharecropping. She played a major role in the NAACP's anti-lynching fundraisers and contributed thousands of dollars to black schools, individuals, organizations, and institutions. She said to Negro women everywhere, "Don't sit down and wait for the opportunities to come, get up and make them." She used her wealth and status to work towards political and economic rights for African Americans and women. Money did not rule Madam CJ Walker, and she gave back with a vengeance.

There are over a hundred Historical Black Colleges and Universities (HBCU) in the United States. One of which

For the Love of Money is Lincoln University, located in Jefferson City, Missouri, my Alma Mater and soon to be my daughter's. It was not until the mid to late 1800's that African Americans got the opportunity to earn a degree at the college level. Lincoln University was founded as Lincoln Institute in 1816 by veterans of the 62 and 65 Regiment United States, Colored Troops. The former soldiers intended to provide an education to African Americans through the combining of academics and labor, in the industrial school model characteristic of Booker T. Washington's influential Tuskegee Institute. Under the Morrill Act of 1890, Missouri designated the school as a land-grant university, emphasizing agriculture, mechanics and teaching. Here is a prime example of African Americans giving and sacrificing for black people, not wanting any monetary gain in return.

Other black philanthropists include Ray Charles who boycotted his own state because of segregation and gave over twenty million dollars to HBCUs. Michael Jordan donated several million dollars to keep the doors of Hales

For the Love of Money
Franciscian High School open, on the south side of Chicago. Denzel and Paulette Washington recently donated over a million dollars to the Historically Black Wiley College. Alonzo Mourning and his wife Tracy donated over seven million dollars to non-profits that serve at-risk children.

I often joke about how I will only marry a woman who earns at least seventy-five thousand dollars a year or else I am going to have a prenuptial agreement. A female colleague of mine is quick to say, yeah, so you can keep her away from your Probation Officer salary, and cracks up. While it is easy to focus too much on monetary gain, Timothy cautions us against the temptation to be a gain seeker. Paul let Timothy know that piety is not good enough; you have to have piety and contentment. Piety means goodness, faithfulness, and Godliness. If you have holiness, gratification, happiness and satisfaction, you have contentment, giving you the ability to not be a gain seeker. There is nothing wrong with being rich, but desires for riches at any cost strangles contentment.

For the Love of Money

The love of money is the root of all evil, but is not the only thing that can drive a person to do evil deeds. It is not the money itself that is the problem, but the wishing to be rich at any means. The love of money can lead to bitterness, destroys faith and once faith is destroyed, it is followed closely by its companions of temptation, lust, and destruction.

Paul tells Timothy to flee riches and follow after Godliness. He implies if you have God you have true riches. Paul understood that many wicked behaviors grow from the love of money, such as divorce, murder, robbery, forgery, illegal distribution of drugs, prostitution and burglary to name a few. Remember, you cannot take anything with you to your grave. If you are saved, love God, have friends and family to love, who love you, what more can you ask for. Donald Sterling bragged about giving people things. He said in regard to the NBA, who gives it to them? Does someone else give it to them? Who makes the game? Do I make the game or do they make the game? Are there thirty owners who created the league?

For the Love of Money

What a pious, arrogant, and haughty person, you should never ever want to be like that.

Chapter 11
Put a Ring on It

A certain man had two sons and the younger of them said to his father, give me the portion of goods that falleth to me. He divided unto them his living, and not many days after the younger son gathered all together, and took his journey into a far country, and there wasted his substance with riotous living. When he came to himself, he said, how many hired servants of my father's have bread enough to spare and I perish with hunger? I will arise and go to my father, and will say unto him, father, I have sinned against heaven, and before thee, and am no more worthy to be called thy son. Make me as one of thy hired servants and he arose, and came to his father. When he was yet a great way off, his father saw him, and had compassion, and ran, and fell on his neck, and kissed him. The son said unto him, "Father, I have sinned against heaven, and in thy sight, and am no more worthy to be called thy son." The father said to his servants, "Bring forth the best robe, and put it on him; and put a ring on his hand, and shoes on his feet, and bring hither the fatted calf, and kill it, and let us

Put a Ring on It

eat, and be merry. For this my son was dead, and is alive again, he was lost, and is found" (Luke 15:11-32).

The tradition of a man and woman binding their marriage through wedding bands upon the completion of vows by placing a ring on the left finger is rich in symbolism dating back to ancient times. The symbolism of wedding rings began with the ancient Egyptians, who braided papyrus into jewelry, believing that a circle represented timelessness, with rings binding two people in eternal love and life. Placing the ring on the third finger of the left hand stems from the ancient Egyptian and Roman belief that the vein of this finger travels to the heart, referred to as vena amoris, meaning vein of love.[46]

Beyonce said, "All the single ladies put your hands up, I'm up on him, he's up on me, don't pay him any attention. Don't treat me to the things of the world, I'm not that kind of girl, your love is what I prefer, what I deserve." In other words, I may be of the world, but I ain't a whore.

Put a Ring on It

Don't treat me any kind of way, if you want me, put a ring on it.[26]

A ring symbolizes unity, wisdom, love and fidelity. It represents trustworthiness, reliability, loyalty and being in agreement. Though God hates when you do the wrong thing, you have an advocate with the father. That does not mean you have a license to mistreat, disrespect, and cause harm to others. Though God is married to the backslider, there is no once a Christian always a Christian. You may fall several times, but he who is spiritual is obligated to pray and restore you. If with the knowledge of God you deliberately violate people, there remaineth no more sacrifices for you. In other words, to know right and to do wrong is not pleasant in the eyesight of God. So, when you are tempted to do the wrong thing, resist the devil and he will flee.

You are an epistle written and read of all men and God does not take lightly your desire to take a stand for him. Satan wants you to think like him, that it is okay to sin as long as you repent later. It would be easy for you to be promiscuous and later apologize, but in many cases the damage will have already been done. Such immoral behavior can be a contributing factor to mental, emotional and spiritual decay. Some people suffer organic emotional impairment, meaning they are born with mental illness or disease, but I'm convinced that many people become illogical, irrational and distressed because they refuse to give their life to the Lord, and try to work things out on their own. Our fragile body was not made to take such mental and emotional abuse.

Alcohol, marijuana, crack cocaine, and meth users like the pleasure it gives them. Criminologists have proven that in the beginning people do not like the taste of alcohol, marijuana or meth but learn to like it. At the start, people do not like drugs, but in seeking pleasure and avoiding pain, they lose control. For you, Christ makes himself available to minister to your every need.

Put a Ring on It

The parable of the prodigal son is in the Bible to mentor, guide, teach and advise you. It is designed to compel you to minister to friends, meet the need of those whom nothing has been prepared, and help reform people's lives. What role are you playing in bringing people to a state of repentance, reform and service? If you really love the Lord, you should always be drawn to his instructions and conduct yourself in a Godly way. He takes great pleasure in our conversion; as a matter of fact he gets more joy out of one converted person than he does the ninety-nine who are already converted.

Just like the prodigal son, the drug dealer, thief, gang banger, and murderer have some redeeming qualities. Those of you who are blessed with your right mind should be leading the search for those who are lost. What man that has a hundred sheep, loses one, does not leave the ninety-nine and go try to find it? What woman who has ten diamond rings, who loses one, does not get a candle out and try to find it? Not only does she go and find it, but

Put a Ring on It

when she finds it, she tells everybody so they can rejoice with her.

Notice that the prodigal son thinks about what he will say to his father, repents, acknowledges that he is wrong, and is not worthy to be his son. He does not deny the relationship, but knows his father can shut the door in his face. His father called for a robe, the garment of princes and great men, and put a ring on his hand. The ring was a signet-ring with arms of the family, sealing that he belonged to the family. God has done the same for you, put a ring on you, making you part of the royal family.

Chapter 12
These Three Words

"Moses lifted up the serpent in the wilderness; even so must the Son of Man be lifted up: that whosoever believeth in him should not perish, but have eternal life. For God so loved the world, that he gave his only begotten Son, that whosoever believeth in him should not perish, but have everlasting life. For God sent not his Son into the world to condemn the world; but that the world through him might be saved. He that believeth in him is not condemned: but he that believeth not is condemned already, because he hath not believed in the name of the only begotten Son of God. And this is the condemnation, that light is come into the world, and men loved darkness rather than light, because their deeds were evil. For every one that doeth evil hateth the light, neither cometh to the light, lest his deeds should be reproved. But he that doeth truth cometh to the light that his deeds may be made manifest, that they are wrought in God" (John 3:14-21).

These Three Words

Passion is a powerful thing and can be defined as a strong and barely controllable emotion. Barely controllable meaning, difficult to manage, hard to control and tough to keep under wraps. There are many other emotions, such as joy, sadness, hate and love to name a few. While the Bible proclaims you can have joy everlasting, some criminal behaviors are committed out of passion. The crime of passion most intriguing to me as a criminal justice practitioner is what the Uniform Crime Report terms triangular homicide, what I call the cheating spouse scenario. Triangular homicide can be defined as a love triangle ending in the death of one, two or three people.

In Memphis, in 1884, the conductors of the Chesapeake and Ohio Railroad Company said, "Get up and give your seat to that white man and go to the Jim Crow car." Despite the 1874 Civil Rights Act banning discrimination on the basis of race, creed, or color, in theaters, hotels, transports, and other public accommodations, several railroad companies defied this congressional mandate and racially segregated its passengers.

These Three Words

In her autobiography Ida B. Wells wrote, "I refused, saying that the forward car was a smoker, and as I was in the ladies' car, I proposed to stay. The conductor tried to drag me out of the seat, but the moment he caught hold of my arm I fastened my teeth in the back of his hand. I had braced my feet against the seat in front and was holding to the back, and as he had already been badly bitten he didn't try it again by himself. He went forward and got the baggage man and another man to help him and of course they succeeded in dragging me out." As a civil rights activist, no one showed more love and passion for her people than Ida B. Wells who fought for African American rights her entire life.[36]

Love is profoundly tender, a passionate affection, a feeling of warm personal attachment and a deep affection. Love is Boaz and Ruth. Boaz, known as a man of standing, and in modern terms a woman might say he was a sight for sore eyes, good to look upon, and arguably, he felt love at first sight for Ruth. In a court of law, the argument would be won beyond a reasonable doubt. The Bible informs us that

These Three Words

Boaz asked in his manly voice, "Who's this fine woman over here?" He requested that Ruth continue to glean in his field, and helped her far beyond the law. Boaz was not playing, as Ruth was allowed to gather extra barley.

Ruth on the other hand was not messing around either. With my greatest Holy Ghost imagination, while batting her eyes Ruth said, "Boaz why do I find favor in your eyes?" Why did Ruth ask brotha Boaz that same question, not once, not twice, but three times? Ruth then asked, "May I continue to have favor in your eyes my Lord?" If a woman ever referred to me as Lord, I'm searching for a preacher that day, and headed to the altar the following day. A woman can refer to me as Lord if she wants to, but I must warn her, if she does, it's all over. Ruth further stated that Boaz, put her at ease. What? What woman says that today, none that I know off. Brothas, if you have a woman like that you had better hold on tight because she is the catch of a lifetime.

These Three Words

Boaz was smooth, he said come on over here woman and have some of my bread and vinegar. You offer a woman of the twenty-first century bread and vinegar and she will look at you like you are crazy, and demand a steak, some ribs, fried chicken, greens, corn bread, macaroni and cheese and a diet coke.

Ruth's love for Naomi was so strong that it began to lessen Naomi's bitterness toward God, and caused her to change. Love is kind, patient, and long suffering. It is not like the love of Jim Jones of Jamestown who murdered over nine hundred people, David Koresh who sexually abused twelve-year-old girls, John Wayne Gacy, the Son of Sam and Ted Bundy.

The love between a man and a woman calls for all five love languages to be spoken if necessary; acts of service, words of affirmation, quality time, gifts and physical touch. If most of the time you are concerned about yourself, it is important to remember that the love languages are not meant to be selfishly used, but are to minister to your partner.

God loves you so much that he gave his only begotten son, did not take, but gave. Jesus gave his life so that you would have everlasting life. What a great day it is going to be when you see Jesus. For the dead in Christ shall rise first, then those who remain shall be caught up to meet him in the air, surpassing the tribulation period to the Beama Seat of Christ, judgment day for the Christian.

You are promised a crown of victory, authority, responsibility, and heavenly treasure with eternal value and security, and special blessings for overcoming special trials and tests. You are promised an incorruptible crown, crowns of glory, righteousness, life and exultation. If, you can just say These Three Words to the Lord, "I Love You."

Chapter 13
Things

In several Civil Rights Cases in 1883, the Supreme Court ruled that Equal Protection under the Law applied only to state action, not to segregation by privately owned businesses. In his majority opinion, Justice Joseph Bradley wrote, it would be running the slavery argument into the ground to make it apply to every act of discrimination which a person may see fit to make as to guests he will entertain, or as to the people he will take into his coach, cab, car, concert or theatre. In his dissenting opinion, Justice John Harlan, the only justice of the nine to disagree wrote, Congress was attempting to overcome the refusal of the states to protect the rights denied to African-Americans that white citizens took as their birthright.

It is a great thing when a person stands up for what is right. Discrimination is never right whether it is age, race, gender, sexual orientation, or economically related. Thank God that he is no respecter of person. In a way, Malcolm

Things X was right when he said a man who stands for nothing will fall for anything.[17] He also said be peaceful, be courteous, obey the law, respect everyone; but if someone puts his hand on you, send him to the cemetery, but God says only what you do for Christ is gonna last. So, I ask you, what are you fighting for? Are you into things, diamond rings, cars, designer suits? What profits a man to gain the whole world and lose his soul?

Justice Harlan, a Caucasian man could see what the system was doing to black people, but eight other justices could not. Yes, eight other Supreme Court Justices voted against the Civil Rights Act of 1875 and could not see that Jim Crow was wrong. Justices of the highest court in the land did not view segregation as wrong. God desires for black people to help Caucasian people and white people to help African American people. Thank God for Thurgood Marshall, the first African American Supreme Court Justice, and lead counsel in Brown V. Board of Education.

In his study of the Philadelphia Negro, W.E.B. Dubois talks about the social ills of black people, compares the Southern Negro with the Northern Negro, and found that the Southern Negros suffered from anomie. Though modern criminologist such as Emile Durkheim is credited with studying the concept of anomie, Dubois considered it long before Durkheim. Anomie means a state of normlessness, which many blacks experienced after the emancipation proclamation. Dubois concluded that more crime was committed by blacks in the South due to a lack of opportunity afforded the African Americans in the North.[15]

Dubois documented that black folk suffered from social structure and strain even before the great Robert Merton theorized it. Social structure and strain theory argues that folks are not bad, but commit criminal acts because of the way society is structured, institutionalized racism, discrimination, and a lack of opportunity to achieve the American dream.

Things

Way back in 1899, Dubois found that crime committed by African Americans declined when there was an improvement in their level of education and employment. He further found as blacks moved toward equal status with their white counter parts their criminal behavior declined. Could this be why the devil doesn't want our young black youth to be educated? Could this be why Satan wants to keep the African American men at a low level of employment?

Dubois wrote about this in the late nineteen century, but you don't read about his contributions. What am I saying? His writings are a part of American history too. He was a criminologist, sociologist, historian and civil rights activist. The question continues to be asked if we need Affirmative Action and Historical Black Colleges and Universities, without a doubt.

The great Dubois had a Christian Creed: Everybody is equal: black folk, white folk, Mexican folk, Asian folk, and people should not be judged by the color of their skin.

He said this way before the great Dr. Martin Luther King Jr. My point is there was a time when people stood for meaningful things. Ida B. Wells, journalist, newspaper owner, and author, documented the extent of lynching. She actually risked her life to publicly record how often, why, and who was most likely to be a victim of lynching. She reported that black men often times were victims due to successful performance in business, not acting inferior to white folk and being falsely accused of raping white women. Where are the Ida B. Wells of today, the virtuous woman? So many of our women today are consumed with the designer suit, diamond ring, and are self-centered and selfish.

Not all women are consumed with themselves. Take for example Michelle Alexander, former racial discrimination litigator and law clerk for Supreme Court Justice Harry Blackman. Alexander argues in her book, *The New Jim Crow: Mass Incarceration in the Age of Colorblindness* that Jim Crow still exists. Black men are imprisoned on drug charges at a rate twenty to fifty times greater than white men. According to Alexander, white men are more likely to engage in drug crimes than people of color.[1]

Ida B. Wells made significant contributions on a train well before the great Rosa Parks did on a bus. The Tennessee Supreme Court said in Well's case, we think it is evident that the purpose of the defendant in error was to harass with a view to this suit, and that her persistence was not in good faith to obtain a comfortable seat for the short ride. Sold out by her African American attorney, Wells turned to a Caucasian attorney to help her get justice.

You may have a lot of stuff, but when you add it up what does it mean? We often make a big fuss over material possessions and things that do not contribute to our ability to love. Money can dress you up, but when you take your clothes off, is the loneliness still there? Though your money can take you where you want to go, in the darkness of the night, Jesus is the only one who knows your trouble and can bring you peace. Things fade away, disappear, rust and evaporate, but Jesus is love everlasting.

In his Sermon on the Mount, Jesus speaks to the disciples concerning God's kingdom and righteousness. He tells them to let their behavior be governed by righteousness and unless their righteousness exceeds that of the Scribes and Pharisees they would not enter the kingdom of heaven. In other words, there is a standard of righteousness. Christ compassionately is saying, realize how blessed you are. You don't have to worry about white and black water fountains, segregated theaters and buses and lynching. Do not let your greatest aspiration be purchasing a car, home and clothing. Lay not up for yourself treasures on this earth like the rich young ruler, but do those things that get you closer to the kingdom of heaven.

It is important to understand that whether you are black, white, red or blue, you are not seeking the kingdom of God and do not have his righteous character when you are discriminating against someone because of their race, creed or color. You are not seeking God's righteousness if you are committing hate crimes against people, and you definitely are not going to see Jesus if you are mistreating people because of their sexual orientation.

The Kingdom of God is like a man on a far journey delivering goods to his servants demanding them to turn a profit; to which much is given much is required. God expects you to take your talents and use them for his glory. When people are sick, he expects you to help them get well. When people are naked, he expects you to clothe them. When people are in prison, he expects you to minister to them. When people are thirsty, he expects you to give them drink, and when people are hungry he expects you to feed them.

Chapter 14
Can Anything Good Come Out of Nazareth

The day following Jesus would go forth into Galilee, and find Philip, and saith unto him, follow me. Now Philip was of Bethsaida, the city of Andrew and Peter. Philip found Nathanael, and saith unto him, we have found him, of whom Moses in the law, and the prophets, did write, Jesus of Nazareth, the son of Joseph. And Nathanael said unto him, can there any good thing come out of Nazareth? Philip saith unto him, Come and see. Jesus saw Nathanael coming to him, and saith unto him; behold an Israelite indeed, in who is no guile. Nathanael saith unto him, whence knowest thou me? Jesus answered and said unto him, before that Philip called thee, when thou were under the fig tree, I saw thee. Nathanael answered and saith unto him, Rabbi, thou art the Son of God; thou art the King of Israel. Jesus answered and said unto him, because I said unto thee, I saw thee under the fig tree, believest thou? Thou shalt see greater things than these. And he saith unto him, verily, verily, I say unto you, hereafter ye shall see

Can Anything Good Come Out of Nazareth

heaven open, and the angels of God ascending and descending upon the Son of man (John 1:43-51).

"You," said the doctor to the patient, "are in terrible shape. You've got to do something about it. First, tell your wife to cook more nutritious meals. Stop working like a dog. Also, inform your wife you're going to make a budget, and she has to stick to it. And have her keep the kids off your back so you can relax. Unless there are some changes like that in your life, you'll probably be dead in a month." "Doc", the patient said, "this would sound more official coming from you. Could you please call my wife and give her those instructions?" When the fellow got home, his wife rushed to him. "I talked to your doctor," she said. "Poor man, you've only got thirty days to live."[11]

In many instances we are harder on ourselves than the Lord. We lock ourselves in our own prison, play the role of the victim, sing unto ourselves a who done me wrong song, all to make ourselves feel good. We play the victim role though many times we are the victimizer, lying,

Can Anything Good Come Out of Nazareth

cheating and stealing, yielding to Satan whose job it is to steal, kill and destroy. Remember, every man is tempted, when he is drawn away of his own lust, enticed, and chooses to do wrong. In other words, we sometimes lure, entice, bait and injure ourselves and others, in disobedience to the Lord.

No man is beyond the possibility of change and God desires for us to take control of our life. To take control of your life, you have to be willing to be transformed by the renewing of your mind. If you need to change, but do not want to change, it means you are being dishonest, cannot be trusted, are deceitful and in a state of disloyalty. You are in a state that is synonymous to being a liar. Revelations states, "The fearful, unbelieving, and all liars, shall have their part in the lake of fire. When you accept Christ as your Lord and Savior, old things are passed away, behold all things have become new." I don't know about you, but if I need to change, I want to change. I've learned not to try to control things that I have no control

Can Anything Good Come Out of Nazareth

over. I can't even control myself without the help of the Lord.

In the last days of Judah, God told Jeremiah repeatedly not to pray for the nation because he would not listen to their pleas. "Therefore, do not pray for this people, nor lift up a cry or prayer for them, nor make intercession; for I will not hear you," God said. There was only one option left for the nation and that was death.

The woman at the well professed "Come and see a man who told me everything about myself." She was not excited about the possibility of marrying her sixth husband, as Jesus discerned that the fifth man she was with was not hers. She was excited about her spiritual change which took place due to the truth shared with her by Christ. This similar change is what Dr. Martin Luther King Jr. was hoping for when he quoted William Cullen Bryant, "Truth crushed to earth shall rise again."

Can Anything Good Come Out of Nazareth

Used in his 1957 "Give us the ballot" speech, Dr. King decreed, "Truth ain't going anywhere, give us the ballot for basic rights, lynching, and we will place judges on the benches of the South who will do justly and love mercy." The woman at the well was excited about the truth Jesus shared with her about her lifestyle and it changed.

For the possibility of change, look no further than Ferguson, Missouri where some good changes have been made. Judge Roy Richter was replaced with the Honorable Ronald Brockmeyer. A judge's approach matters. Ferguson was profiting off the backs of African American citizens through racial profiling. Judge Brockmeyer slashed fines and jailed no one for minor infractions. That was a significant change in the administration of justice in Ferguson.

After all David's indiscretions, sleeping with Bathsheba, and putting Uriah on the front line, he asked the Lord to make known his end, the measure of his days, that he may know how frail he was. David understood that his days

Can Anything Good Come Out of Nazareth

were numbered, he was fragile, and life was a vapor. Therefore, he found himself praising and magnifying God, entering into his gates with thanksgiving and into his courts with praise. Saying great is the Lord and greatly to be praised, in the city of our God and the mountain of his holiness. David said, "I will bless the Lord at all times, his praises shall continually be in my mouth, my soul shall make a boast in the Lord, the humble shall hear and be glad, O magnify the Lord with me and let us exalt his name together." (Psalms 34:1-3)

John teaches us that Jesus had been down by the Jordan where John was baptizing. Jesus goes to the region of Galilee instead of Judea or Jerusalem where all the prestige and power was. It would be like going to Bloomington, Illinois instead of St. Louis or Chicago. For some reason Jesus goes to lowly Galilee; once he is there, he impresses on Phillip to change his ways. Phillip finds Nathan and tells him that he found Jesus of Nazareth, the son of Joseph and the one who the prophets have written

Can Anything Good Come Out of Nazareth
about. Nathan's response was, Jesus of Nazareth? You mean Jesus of Judea or Jerusalem.

Nazareth was the home village of Mary, the mother of Jesus, and the place where the angel Gabriel announced the birth of Jesus. Nazareth, a small agricultural village, with little economic importance, was populated with Jewish people. Though it was the place where Gabriel announced the birth of Jesus, it had a negative connotation.

Nathan's perception is important because it is very similar to the way some Americans view each other, churches, African Americans, Caucasians and vice versa. If Nathan would have kept this attitude, he would have missed out on the blessings of God.

Take note of how Phillip did not try to explain to Nathan the greatness of Jesus. Phillip understood Jesus was king of kings, Lord of Lords, Alpha and Omega, the beginning and the end. He does not get sidetracked into a discussion

Can Anything Good Come Out of Nazareth

of how great or lack thereof Nazareth is. He simply says, "Come see."

Nathanael believes that nothing good could possibly come out of Nazareth. I don't care if you are the black sheep of your family, you ought to be encouraging yourself by asking, can anything good come out of Nazareth. I often tell my students, if a country boy from Festus, Missouri can be successful, you can too. I may phrase it in the aforementioned way, but what I'm really saying is, come see a man who saved me, delivered me and set me free. You too can be changed, you don't have to say anything, simply accept Christ and people will begin to see you change.

You don't have to tell people how great you are and give them all your accolades. There is always someone more knowledgeable than you. You don't have to tell people how awesome your church is, as though it is Holy Ghost headquarters. There is always a church that has more money, programs and a better looking edifice. What you

Can Anything Good Come Out of Nazareth should be concerned with is, does the spirit of God abide in your church, are souls given the opportunity to repent, and does salvation and deliverance take place there. No matter how lowly a place may seem, you should never be ashamed to bring people to where Jesus is. You can let your neighbor, co-worker, family and everyone know that you've found a savior and his name is Jesus. If anyone asks, can anything good come out of Nazareth, like Phillip, you tell them come see man.

Let me end by saying, it is a blessing to be shepherded by charismatic, delivered, honest and trustworthy pastors. Joseph Brown was born and raised in the projects of Chicago and Vicky Brown is from East St. Louis, two of the toughest cities in the United States of America. They are not just my pastors, but two of my best friends. To be up under their ministry and to watch how they practice what they preach has really been a blessing. I am biased, but there could not possibly be two more fun loving, down to earth people with such great senses of humor. I love you so much.

Chapter 15
Muzzle Not the Ox

Let the elders that rule well be counted worthy of double honor, especially they who labor in the word and doctrine. For the scripture saith thou shalt not muzzle the ox that treaded out the corn. The laborer is worthy of his reward. (I Timothy 5:17-18)

Integrity Deliverance Church recently celebrated its twenty-first church anniversary, where I have been a member for twenty years. I thank God for the opportunity to honor my pastors with the preaching of the word each anniversary Sunday. It gives me an opportunity to be used by the Lord, but most importantly it is an occasion to tell them how much I love them and to say thanks for their unconditional love. Yes, if you have pastors who are sober minded and not double minded, you should bless them every chance you get.

In Broadus and Stanfield's fourth edition of *On the Preparation and Delivery of Sermons,* Chapter 5 entitled

"The Text" states, "To let the needs of the congregation determine the choice of text." If preaching is to meet the needs of humanity, then texts should be chosen that meet these needs. Sermons should not just be subject centered, but person centered. Texts should be selected to fulfill all of the needs of the people.[7]

On church anniversary day, week or month, however your church does it, it should be primarily dedicated to the pastors. The Subject that meets the congregation's needs on that day should be one that honors the pastors. When you honor your pastor, you are honoring God.

You should honor your pastors not because of how they look, but honor them because of their labor and work's sake. Pastors caution, counsel and advise you, urge you to duty, and are responsible for shepherding you into heaven. Pastoring is no joke. My pastor, Joe Brown, worked third shift as a criminal justice practitioner for over fifteen years. He would get off work at seven o'clock Sunday mornings and preach his heart out every Sunday until his recent retirement from the McLean County Juvenile Detention Center. He is now pastoring full time. Don't esteem pastors for who they are as people, nor the humanistic things they do to please themselves, but for the work of God. Co-Pastor Vicky Brown has not been concerned about how many diamond rings she's received over the years, but whether she has been pleasing to the Lord.

One in five Americans has reported that religion does not play an important role in their lives. In a recent NBC/WSJ poll, twenty-one percent of respondents said that religion is not that important to their lives. This is the highest percentage since the poll began asking participants about their focus on faith in 1997. The poll shows that these less religious Americans are mostly men, make over seventy-five thousand dollars per year, and are under the age of thirty-five. Implying that money, invincibility and gender are driving forces to a lack of holiness.

Although a poll can't tell us who is a Christian, it can infer who God is important to. More than half of Americans still place a major emphasis on their faith. Thirteen percent of respondents in the poll said that religion is the most important aspect of their lives, and forty-one percent said it is very important. What stands out is that the forty-one percent that said it's very important should have said it is most important. Pastors truly have a challenging job.

The Ox is a fitting symbol of the pastor because of its strength and labor. Pastors have to be strong in the Lord and in the power of his might. They work when everybody else is asleep, beat out the gospel truths, make doctrine clear, plain and evident to the understanding of men. The ultimate aim of the pastor is the welfare of man.

The book of Luke gives two examples of testimonies that support honorable maintenance being given to those who are ministers of the gospel. The two examples are Moses and Christ. In sending the disciples out to preach the word, the laborer is worthy of his hire. He is to go not from house to house, but to those that receive the gospel. The preacher is to depend upon those who receive the gospel for subsistence. Those who minister the gospel should not frown upon how they are welcomed, nor be afraid of being troublesome, but eat and drink heartily such things as are given. For whatever kindness you show to the preacher is but a small return for the kindness and glad tidings of peace they bring.

Obey them that have the rule over you, and submit yourselves, for they watch for your souls, as they that must give account. In other words, the preacher has to do their job with joy, and not with grief, for that is unprofitable for you. To give an account means pastors have to explain their decisions concerning the sheep. If the pastor mistreats you, God will discipline him or her. The pastor's mission is the welfare of the church.

The people of God are to respect and honor their pastor. When the church rebels it hinders progress. A church cannot possibly be of one accord, of one heart, and of one soul for the Lord unless every member has the proper attitudes and actions of respect for the pastor. God is no respecter of persons, all believers are equal, but we're ordained to different roles. As much as some folks might desire the leadership role in the church, it's clearly bestowed by the Lord upon the pastor. Pride filled believers can turn congregations into board-run churches, domineering man or woman run churches, and devil-run churches. God is not the author of confusion, but of peace, and all things should be done decently and in order. Let's hold our pastors, their wives, and children in fervent prayer every day. Let's seek to encourage them often, stand up for them whenever anyone would seek to tear them down and love them as Jonathan loved David.

Receiving the *Adjunct Faculty of the Year Award* from Rob Widmer, President of Heartland Community College.

My friend Ryan and his boys, before a Cardinals game.

Some friends and members of our church family.

Above: Family at Mom's retirement party.

Below: Four influential Pastors.

From left to right: Whitney (daughter), Annette (Mom), Paul (Dad), and Dewhitt II (son).

Sister Stephanie Thomas and I, present with the Lord.

Friends I grew up with from the neighborhood. (top left image)
Juliana's birthday, from left to right: Dewhitt II, Juliana, and Dewhitt (top right image)

High school reunion, from left to right: Laura, Anthony, Ken, and Dewhitt (bottom image)

Church Anniversary, from left to right: Pastor Vicky, Diane, Dewhitt and Pastor Joe

Panel Discussion at Heartland Community College

Chapter 16
Throwing Stones

Repentance, salvation, and deliverance are the three things God desires for all mankind. He convicts, saves, sets us free and then instructs us on how to grow. John puts it like this: Jesus went unto the Mount of Olives, and early in the morning he came again into the temple, and all the people came unto him; and he sat down, and taught them. The Scribes and Pharisees brought unto him a woman taken in adultery. When they had set her in the midst, they said unto him, master, this woman was taken in adultery, in the very act. Moses in the law commanded us, that such should be stoned, but what sayest thou? This they said, tempting Jesus to accuse him. Jesus stooped down, and with his finger wrote on the ground, as though he heard them not. So when they continued asking him, he lifted up himself, and said unto them, he that is without sin, let him cast the first stone at her. Again he stooped down, wrote on the ground, and they which heard it, being convicted by their own conscience, went out one by one. Jesus was left alone, and the woman standing in the midst. When Jesus

Throwing Stones

had lifted up himself, and saw none but the woman, he said unto her, woman, where is thine accusers? Hath no man condemned thee? She said, no man, Lord. Jesus said unto her, neither do I condemn thee. Go and sin no more (John 8:1-11).

A man working in the produce department was asked by a lady if she could buy a half a head of lettuce. He replied, "Half a head? Are you serious? God grows these in whole heads and that's how we sell em!"

"You mean that after all the years I've shopped here you won't sell me a half-a-head of lettuce?"

"Look lady, if you like I'll ask the manager."

"Well I would appreciate that," said the woman.

So the young man marched to the front of the store and said to the manager, "You won't believe this, there's a lame brained idiot of a lady back there who wants to know if she can buy a half a head of lettuce." The man noticed the manager gesturing, and turned around to see the lady standing behind him. After seeing that the lady was standing behind him, the man said to his manager, "And this nice lady was wondering if she could buy the other half a head of lettuce."[41]

For biblical evidence of stoning look no further than the laws of the Old Testament. After bringing his people out of bondage God wanted to speak to them. They were to come to Mount Sinai, but observe the boundaries of Mount Sinai or be stoned. Leviticus teaches that idol worshipers and those who turned their head to it were stoned. "If any people of the land do any ways hide their eyes from the man, when he giveth of his seed unto Molech, and kill him not, then I will set my face against that man, his family, and will cut him off, and all that go a whoring after him." It is safe to say that it was dangerous to be a whore in the Old Testament. However, before you throw stones at the Christians of that day, ask yourself if you idolize anything, houses, land, children, wife, or husband.

Deuteronomy instructs the Christian to put no one before God almighty. In the Old Testament we find that spies were sent to listen to the people's idolatrous tendencies and to see if they put others before God. After a trial and conviction for idolatry, you were stoned to death. Your relative might have cast the first stone, and then everybody else stoned you, dad, mom, brother, and sister; family relations did not matter.

Another example of stoning occurred when the people of God lost the battle to small Ai. They were smote by Ai because there was sin amongst them. Joshua beckoned Achan to tell what he had done. Achan committed the trespass and caused the entire nation to suffer, all because he wanted a shag carpet and a few dollars. He along with his children was stoned and their bodies were burned.

Of course, we cannot forget about Stephen who was stoned for preaching the gospel of Jesus Christ. Stephen tells the Lord, "Lay none of this at their charge," just as Jesus on the cross said, "Father forgive them for they know not what they do."

Throwing Stones

Here Jesus is on the Mount of Olives where several key events in the life of Christ take place, including where he ascended to heaven, and today serves as a major site of Christian pilgrimage. As Jesus is teaching, here come the Scribes and the Pharisees and they say to Jesus, we have this whore that committed adultery, caught in the very act and the law says she should be stoned.

The Scribes and Pharisees, the bible scholars of that day, pulled the law out on Jesus. I'm convinced that they sometimes forgot that in the beginning was the Word, the Word was God and the Word was with God, and Jesus is the Word. The Word was made flesh, dwelt among men, and came that we might have life and life more abundantly. What am I saying? The Scribes and Pharisees didn't know who Jesus was. Jesus said, "My father bears witness of me" and they asked him who his father was. Wise, intelligent, smart and judicious Christians, but education will make a fool out of you.

Throwing Stones

Have you ever met someone who can't see any of your positive traits, constantly finds fault, and puts you down rather than builds you up? The Scribes' and Pharisees' problem was their way of thinking. Herein is the reason why no matter how you were born, the Bible declares that you have to be born again, and be transformed by the renewing of your mind.

To be a good witness you must pay close attention to your thoughts, recognize the risk in your thinking, and then use new thinking. You must replace those derogative thoughts with thinking that will help build people up. Furthermore, you must always recognize what you are thinking, and identify your attitude, feelings and beliefs that are destructive. You cannot be conformed to this world, but must be transformed by the renewing of your mind so that you can know what is good, acceptable, and perfect in the eyesight of God.

Christians especially should have no desire to model the Corinthian church, a church that liked to find fault, was influenced by the social movement of the day, and made excuses to mistreat others. The church at Corinth misused the scriptures to commit fornication, drink and be merry, and used the word of God as an excuse to justify their sinful behavior. However, before you criticize the Corinthian church, when was the last time you threw a stone?

Paul told the Corinthian church to build each other up, don't throw stones, and pray for your fellow man. Let me take this opportunity to clarify what Paul meant by "All things are not expedient." To many Christians, they think this means if it is not convenient for them, they don't have to do it. What Paul meant was you should not govern yourself according to societal beliefs that violate God's word. For example, you should never condone the murder of police officers, or the murder of unarmed African American men.

You can't live in a glass house and throw stones. You will be judged the same way you judge and measured the same way you are measured. If you search to find fault with others, God will search to find fault with you. All humans have flaws and judgment is to be loving, kind and longsuffering. You can't look at the speck in someone else's eye and not see the boulder in your eye. If you do this God calls you uncharitable, mean spirited, heartless and spiteful. Always remember, as a man thinks in his heart so is he and from the abundance of the heart the mouth speaketh.

My prayer is that the Lord would remind you where you come from, to not think more of yourself than you ought, and to always show love, kindness and mercy. Let us show compassion for the poor, children and families crossing the border into the United States of America. I pray that we would take a stand against police brutality and hatred for the police while dealing with the police shootings of unarmed black men. We can do this.

Chapter 17
Reserving the Right

Then came Peter to him, and said, Lord, how often shall my brother sin against me, and I forgive him? Till seven times? Jesus saith unto him, I say not unto thee, until seven times, but until seventy times seven (Matthew 18:21-22).

As an African American I am very grateful for all the civil rights leaders and activists of the past, Ida B. Wells, W.E.B. Dubois, Dr. Martin Luther King Jr., Abraham Lincoln, Viola Liuzzo, and Jonathan Myrick Daniels to name a few. These and many more played significant roles in the passage of the Civil Rights Act of 1964. Many of us want to reserve the right to hold on to anger, hatred, and evil thoughts to justify mistreatment of others. Whether you are black, white, Hispanic or Asian, it is not right to discriminate, be a racist and be prejudiced.

Born in 1962, life is much better for me today because of the sacrifices of the aforementioned men and women. Nothing disturbs me more than someone arguing that they pulled themselves up by their own bootstraps, and alone are responsible for their accomplishments. The truth is no one accomplishes anything by themselves, and sometime during your life someone has helped to open a door for you. If someone is within their right to do something, it means they are spiritually or naturally entitled to do it. To reserve something means to conserve, hang on to, hoard, layup, preserve, or retain it. In many cases a person has neither the moral or legal right to behave a certain way. For example, 720 ILCS 5/11-35 of the Illinois Criminal Statute makes adultery illegal.[24] Any person who has sexual intercourse with another not his spouse commits adultery if the behavior is open and notorious or the person is not married and knows that the other person involved in such intercourse is married. 720 ILCS 5/11-40 of the Illinois Criminal Statute makes fornication illegal.[23] Any person who has sexual intercourse with another not his spouse commits fornication if the behavior is open and notorious. In both cases, fornication and adultery are also spiritual violations of God's word. However, I'm convinced that we reserve the right to violate these laws which destroy friendships, marriages, father and son relationships, and mother and daughter relationships.

I once asked a woman what she struggled with most and she said pride. A pride filled person is arrogant, self-centered, and everything is about them. The person also said she struggled with shopping. I asked her if that was a woman thing and she seemed to think it was. She admitted to having clothes in her closet with the price tag on them. We reserve the right to do a whole lot of things that we should not be doing. Women as well as men know when they are being spiritually influenced by Satan, but rather than listen to the inner man, the flesh rules because we have to look good. God said unto Samuel, look not on his countenance, or on the height of his stature because I have refused him, for the Lord seeth not as man seeth, for man looketh on the outward appearance, but God looketh on the heart. So, she is right, it is the trick of the enemy.

Reserving the Right

Herein is the premise of the Islamic State of Iraq and Syria. The word of God is clear; thou shall not kill, but love thy neighbor and enemy. No one should kill in the name of God. ISIS is reserving the right to kill. If a man be overtaken in a fault, ye which are spiritual restore such a one in the spirit of meekness, considering thyself, lest thou also be tempted.

Many people think because they've lived with a person for a length of time they are officially married. The Bible says you should leave and cleave to your wife, you become a husband, it is ordained by God. We cannot reserve the right to sleep with the opposite sex if you are not married to them.

Physical abuse is another area that men reserve the right to do. There was a time in history when a man could legally rape his wife, a time when she was considered property. This obviously was always wrong, but neither has it ever been okay for a woman to reserve the right to hit a man, call him a punk and provoke him to violence. In many cases, abuse is about power and control, and no one wants to be controlled.

One of the most common forms of abuse is an expression of violence by one person against another in the content of an intimate relationship. Research shows that 1.9 million women are assaulted yearly while 3.2 million men are assaulted yearly and 7.4% of these are assaults in domestic situations. Physical abuse is always wrong whether it is committed by a male or female.

Domestic violence is most common in the states of Nevada, South Carolina, Tennessee, Louisiana, Virginia, Texas, New Jersey, and Arizona, states where women are abused the most. Ninety-three percent of murdered women are murdered by men they know. Sixty-three percent were in the context of an intimate partner relationship, and it is most common in police families. In incidents reported by spouses, research by Strauss and Gelles found twenty-seven percent are initiated by men,

Reserving the Right

twenty-four percent by women and forty-nine percent by both partners, reserving the right to abuse.[38]

In regard to police brutality and excessive force, some police are reserving the right to use excessive force against black men and vice versa. According to a recent study by the University of Chicago and Colorado, police officers are more likely to shoot an unarmed black person than any other person, and less likely to shoot an armed white person than any other person.[27] According to a recent study conducted by Florida State University, police are more likely to let white armed suspects go and more likely to shoot unarmed black suspects. Between 2004 and 2008 in Oakland, California, there were forty-five officer shootings, thirty-seven of the people shot were African American, and none were white. The New York Police Department Firearm Discharge Report in 2011 shows that fifty percent of the people fired upon were black, thirty-five percent of the people fired upon were Hispanic, only fifteen percent of the people fired upon were white. Why is it that black people are getting shot more often than

Reserving the Right

anyone else? Could it be that some are reserving the right to shoot them? Could it be because of the color of their skin? God is no respecter of person and we shouldn't be either.

When the disciples asked Jesus who shall be the greatest in the kingdom, it was a question that many have probably thought to themselves at one time or another. I can see people standing at the pearly gates saying, girl I'm gonna get mine, Jesus where's my stuff, where's my robe you promised me, where's my crown you said I was gonna get. Notice how Jesus deals with the disciples. He doesn't tell them who is going to be the greatest, but he mentions two things. He says, you must be converted and become as little children to enter the kingdom. It's almost as if he was saying you better check yourself. While you are at the gate talking loud, you better examine yourself, because you ain't ready.

What was Jesus trying to tell them? Show humility, meekness, and compassion toward your fellow man. Be submissive to your brother, kindhearted toward your enemy and that will make you the greatest in the kingdom. Do not look down upon your brother nor purposely offend people, Jesus implied. You are the salt of the earth, the light of the world, a peculiar person, and woe to the world if they mess with you because it will be like putting a millstone around their neck and throwing themself into the depths of the sea, vengeance is mine saith the Lord. Therefore, Christians should not be easily offended.

Jesus ends by instructing the disciples on offenses. He says that offenses are going to come because of the cunningness of Satan and the weakness of man's heart. Offenses are permitted to come for a wise and holy end. However, the offenses must be reconciled, bound on earth so that it is bound in heaven, loosed on earth so that it is loosed in heaven. God allows it to happen because he wants to know if you are serious about righteousness. Stop holding on to stuff, let it go. What Peter is really asking is how many times must I forgive this fool who

Reserving the Right

keeps offending me? Jesus stressed that we should always be forgiving.

Chapter 18
A Second Chance

And Saul said to David, behold my elder daughter Merab, her will I give thee to wife: only be thou valiant for me, and fight the Lord's battles. For Saul said, let not mine hand be upon him, but let the hand of the Philistines be upon him. David said unto Saul, Who am I? And what is my life, or my father's family in Israel, that I should be son in law to the king? It came to pass at the time when Merab Saul's daughter should have been given to David that she was given unto Adriel the Meholathite to wife. Michal Saul's daughter loved David: and they told Saul, and the thing pleased him (I Samuel 18:17-20).

Jerry Jones, owner and general manager of the Dallas Cowboys football team, came under a great deal of scrutiny for reinstating troubled players like Adam Jones, Tank Johnson and for allowing players like Terrell Owens to play for him. When interviewed by ESPN on *Outside the Lines*, Jones implied that people can change. To highlight his point, he further implied that he himself had

A Second Chance

been given nine lives. Jones went on to suggest that players understand when they've made a mistake, and in some cases they work harder than those who have not; as if to say, to whom much is given, much is required.

In the beginning God created heaven and earth and the earth was without form and void and darkness was on the face of the deep. Prior to this creation was the dispensation of angels when Lucifer was the head angel, rebellion occurred and God started a new period, a second chance.

God created man and everything that he created was good. Fast forward to Adam and Eve in the Garden, they were deceived, got kicked out of the garden, and gone was the dispensation of innocence, ushering in the dispensation of conscience when man comes to know good and evil. Their sin caused God to repent that he made man, destroyed everything by a flood and created government. Abraham and the fourth dispensation came next with the law and grace to follow. God sends his only begotten Son who

A Second Chance

dies on the cross, defeats Satan, and rises from the dead with all power in his hand. Jesus is victorious over death and puts man in the place where he can be redeemed, reclaimed and brought back in good standing, a second chance.

Think it not strange that the 2012 USA Basketball team that won gold at the Olympics called its team the Redeem Team. After being embarrassed in 2008, the team wanted to redeem itself, because there is power in being redeemed. When you've been redeemed by the blood of the Lamb you want the world to know. I don't know about you, but I'm glad I've been redeemed.

I've pointed out a few times how David was given a second chance after putting Uriah on the front line. David is not the only person who has committed adultery and murdered someone over a woman. Therefore, before you get on David, consider whether you have put someone on the front line.

A Second Chance

Jesus told Peter that he would deny him three times before the cock crowed, but knew Peter would repent. This is why Jesus told Peter, when you are converted, minister to my people. So, before you crucify Peter, you should examine yourself to determine how many times you've lied, not been forth coming and not told the truth. Let me remind you that you can tell a lie as well as you can live one. In addition, you are living a lie if you are not living for Jesus.

Paul built churches, ministered the word of God, had sound character, and was steadfast, consecrated, and faithful. He loved the people, and was one of the greatest preachers to ever walk this earth. The aforementioned life can be considered Paul's second life, after stoning Stephen, making havoc on the church, and persecuting Christians. Paul was so evil, Ananias said, "Lord I have heard by many of this man, how much evil he had done to thy saints at Jerusalem."

A Second Chance

If God is into second chances how much the more should man be willing to give his brother a second chance. I'm glad that God gave me a second chance by sending his only begotten Son to die for my sins. O death, where is thy sting? O grave, where is thy victory? Jesus conquered death, hell and the grave, swallowing up death in victory. So when your pastor preaches stop slipping, tipping and dipping, he's trying to save your life. There cannot be a single person on God's green earth that loves sex more than me, but if I have to give it up as a single brotha, so do you. Christians should not be asking, if the world can do it why can't I?

Abstinence prevents teen pregnancy which is the quickest way to poverty. Our young people should be focused on getting their education, going to college, but instead are more focused on getting a boyfriend or girlfriend.

As for the boyfriend girlfriend thing, my children were taught against it, I taught them to believe in marriage. Even if you believed in the boyfriend and girlfriend thing

A Second Chance

why wouldn't you wait until college, I would tell them. I further exhorted, if you attend a college like Lincoln University, a HBCU founded by the 62nd and 65th Colored Infantries, established Lincoln Institute in 1866 for African Americans interested in continuing their education, you are going to meet all kinds of people. Today, Lincoln University is one of the most diverse four year institutions in the state of Missouri. It serves an international student population from twenty-seven countries around the globe, with the highest numbers from Jamaica, Ghana and Tanzania.

If you are a high school student and you believe you cannot do any better, God is saying yes you can and that all things are possible through Jesus Christ our Lord. When teenagers say that they cannot do any better I always think about my mother, my hero, who birthed me at the age of sixteen. As a result of giving birth to me she had many barriers to overcome in her life. She could have aborted me, but thank God she didn't. She would go on to be a very successful childcare provider for *Head Start*, loved by everyone; I get emotional just thinking about her and surely there is a crown in heaven waiting for her. So, do not tell me what you cannot do, with God's help the sky is the limit.

My grandmother Anna Mae Bingham would say to me when I thought I was in love, you can't live on love alone. What she meant was I could not live on hugs and kisses, but she was not referring to the love of God. There's a secular artist who sang what's love got to do with it? You cannot build a career, marital relationship, a friendship or anything that is worth building without love, and second chances have everything to do with love. When it comes to your spouse and friends, if they repent and ask for your forgiveness, if you are a Christian, you must forgive them. Remember, the Bible says that God is love, he so loved the world that he gave his only begotten son, and if you love him, you must keep his commandments, and forgiveness is one of his mandates. God's word says, love thy neighbor and greater love has no man than this that he lay down his life for a friend. Further, love covers all sin, causes you to

A Second Chance

love your enemies, and proclaims, to love them that love you is definitely not extraordinary.

In the word of God, Saul gives David a second chance to become his son-in-law, but the real question was, did Saul really want David to be his son-in-law? It's a situation that prompted David to say let the redeemed of the Lord say so. David knew Saul's motives were not pure, he was supposed to be given Saul's first daughter, but she was given to Adriel. It was a very calculated attempt on Saul's part to provoke David to sin. He wanted David to experience wounded feelings and provoke him to resentment, but David kept his composure, remained calm, showed self control and was able to resist.

Saul proclaims that his daughter Michal loved David and it pleased him. Actually, it did not please Saul that his daughter was getting a good man, but it pleased him that it was a second chance to snare David. Saul knew David could not afford the dowry to purchase his daughter, either by gifts or service, but said he would accept a courageous

A Second Chance

public service, a hundred foreskins of the Philistines, which required mutilated bodies of the Philistines. This was a common practice in ancient war and the number indicated the glory of the victory, but Saul really wanted David dead, all because of the favor of God received by David. Isn't it good to know that God doesn't have the heart that Saul had? David slew the Philistines, the number was doubled to show his respect and attachment to Saul's daughter, and to oblige his crazy potential father-in-law Saul.

Saul did all this and in the end was still afraid of David because David was destined to be used of God. He was purposed by design and so are you, but you will never fulfill your purpose unless you allow the Lord to give you a second chance, and a second opportunity to live for him. This is the occasion you've been waiting on, don't wait any longer. All have sinned and come short of the glory of God. The wages of sin are death, but the gift of God is eternal life through Jesus Christ our Lord. You can either receive the second chance offered by Jesus or continue to

A Second Chance

allow yourself to be deceived by Satan. The Bible declares, the day you hear his voice harden not your heart.

Chapter 19

A Church without Spot or Wrinkle

What should we be doing as Christians and what is the church's ultimate goal, are questions many church members are asking themselves every day.

There are four main bones in every organization. The wish-bone, those wishing somebody would do something about the problem. The jaw-bone represents the people doing a lot of talking but very little else. The knuckle-bone characterizes those who knock everything and the back-bone personifies those who carry the brunt of the load and do most of the work.

Three pastors got together for coffee one day and found all their churches had bat-infestation problems. "I got so mad," said one, "I took a shotgun and fired at them. It made holes in the ceiling, but did nothing to the bats." "I tried trapping them alive," said the second. "Then I drove 50 miles before releasing them, but they beat me back to

A Church Without Spot or Wrinkle

the church." "I haven't had any more problems," said the third. "What did you do?" asked the others.

"I simply baptized and confirmed them," he replied. "I haven't seen them since."[33]

Due to errors introduced among them and their inconsistent walk in Christ, Paul incites the Colossian church to conduct themselves like Christians. Known for their idol worship, unruly, irresponsible, foolish and reckless behavior, the Ephesians had to be established in the truth. The Galatians had to be counseled against being ensnared, easily misled, wavering and be reproved for their lack of integrity.

Craving for Greek philosophy and rhetoric, Apollo's style over Paul, the Corinthians struggled with living for the Lord. Fornication and adultery was at an all time high, contentions, divisions and lawsuits brought by professing Christians was consuming them. They denied the future resurrection, had a 'let's eat and be merry' attitude, had fervor, but abused spiritual gifts.

A Church Without Spot or Wrinkle

Though free from Judaizing influence, the Philippian Church had to be warned of being tainted. In addition, this church had a tendency to have dissention amongst them. Euodias and Syntyche had to be told to work together.

The Thessalonians were a more perfected church with the only issue being mourning those who died in Christ. Relationships among Christians were good, justification by faith was understood, how Christians should behave was discussed and work was being done in preparation for God's arrival.

Paul began all his epistles to the church with a song of praise to God. The song of praise is for redeeming man from sin, and then he gave thanks for this redemption. According to Paul, the Christian's job is to be a light amongst men that they might turn to God. The world will know that we are Christians by our love and hopefully the world will accept, live and serve God. The church consists of Christians who have repented of their sins, love God, walk in love, work on the Lord's behalf, and are expecting

A Church Without Spot or Wrinkle
Christ's return. Those who attend church and live a saved life are imitators of God. These individuals walk in love, give thanks to Christ in all things, are in union with him and reprove sin.

If the church is filled with Christians and they are followers of Christ, what the church should not be is an unclean place. People who have not repented of their sins and who live a life of sin should not be in a leadership position. Individuals who blatantly disregard God's word, and are unwilling to change, should not be in a management position over the sheep of God's pasture. Filthy communicators should not be allowed to lead God's people. People who covet worship the creature rather than the creator, cannot and should not be before the congregation of God. Christians should not be in fellowship with wicked workers, associating with children of unbelief in doctrine or children of disobedience in practice. Saved folk should not let their good deeds be evil spoken of, are sanctified, and operate from the belief

A Church Without Spot or Wrinkle

that sin is darkness and its parent Satan is the prince of darkness.

Though the church of today contains clean and unclean together, still it is termed holy, in reference to her ideal and ultimate destination which is heaven. When the Bridegroom comes, the bride shall be presented to God holy without spot or wrinkle and the evil will be cut off from the body of Christ forever. Not that there are two churches, one bad and good blended together, but one and the same in relation to different times. Right now the church has good and evil together, hereafter with good alone.

The book of Matthew informs us that there are good and bad fish. The net goes out and draws everything, nothing escapes, there is a separation that eventually takes place and in the end there are multitudes who are Christian in name only. Matthew further tells us that the wheat and tares will grow together in the church, false brethren will

A Church Without Spot or Wrinkle
be amongst us, but it is our job to bring them in and it is God's job to save, deliver and sanctify them.

So those servants went out into the highways, and gathered together all as many as they found, both bad and good. The wedding was furnished with guests and when the king came into see the guests, he saw there a man who had not worn a wedding garment. He saith unto him, "Friend, how camest thou in hither not having a wedding garment?" and he was speechless. Then said the king to the servants, "Bind him hand and foot, and take him away and cast him into outer darkness. There shall be weeping and gnashing of teeth, for many are called, but few are chosen" (Matthew 22:10-14).

"Know you not that your bodies are the members of Christ? Shall I then take the members of Christ, and make them the members of a harlot? God forbid. We are members of His body being of his flesh and of his bones" (I Corinthians 6:15-16).

Chapter 20
Jesus the Same Yesterday Today and Forevermore

One night at a revival meeting a young lady was urged to repent. She said "I will seek the Lord tomorrow night." The next evening her mother found that she intended to go to a ball, and she begged her not to go. The young lady said to her mother, "I'm going to that party even if I die" and went upstairs to get dressed. A young man came to take the young lady to the ball, her mother called for her, but she did not answer. The mother went upstairs to her daughter's room and found her sitting before the mirror, putting a ribbon in her hair, but she was a corpse. She waited one night and lost her soul.

The beginning of the year is when everybody's making a New Year's resolution, but Christians should believe in following the word of God to deal with their situations and circumstances on a daily basis. In other words, in order to make change in your life, you should always apply Christian principles and allow the spirit of the Lord to

Jesus the Same Yesterday Today and Forevermore change you when necessary. If the word of God says that you should change something in your life, you should change it quick and in a hurry.

Making a New Year's resolution implies you are going to wait until January 1st of each year to do it; you could be dead by the time the new year rolls around. It infers that if you are doing something detrimental to your body, soul and spirit, you can wait to make the change. I don't know about you, but if I'm doing something that is detrimental to my body, soul or spirit, I want to change it today; I don't have time to wait especially if it is sinful.

You already know from chapter eighteen that all have sinned and fallen short of the glory of God and the wages of sin is death. The reason why is because Isaiah 59:2 says, sin separates us from God. Remember, it's the spirit man that governs everything; how you think, feel and act. There is a sin unto death and that sin unto death is not murder. Yes, there is a greater sin than murder. Not accepting Jesus Christ as your Lord and Savior is the

Jesus the Same Yesterday Today and Forevermore

greatest sin one can commit. You can't enter the kingdom of God unless you do.

If you want to know why people are depressed, drug addicted, alcoholics, prostitutes, and committing all types of sinful behavior, check out their spirit man; take a look at their spiritual life; get a glimpse of their inner man. What people don't understand is that according to the body, soul and spirit teaching, the word of God teaches that the inner man formulates, creates, puts together, constructs and the body carries it out. So, if your inner man is jacked up, it stands to reason that you are going to engage in unethical behavior.

A secular group of the sixties sang a song that said beauty is only skin deep, if you're looking for a lover don't judge a book by its cover, she may be fine on the outside, but so untrue on the inside. God looks upon the heart of man. Our body is the temple of God. Therefore, it is important for us to take care of our physical body. However, physical appearance does not save, deliver or sanctify us. Psalm

Jesus the Same Yesterday Today and Forevermore 149:4 says that he will beautify the meek with salvation. Some women have their weave, five hundred dollar purses, and makeup on, look and smell good, and are going straight to hell. Some men have their tailor made suits, uptown fade haircuts, driving their Cadillac and living out the trunk of their car. Women don't be deceived; these men are headed straight to hell too. Salvation adorns the Christian with faith, hope, joy and peace. Without faith it is impossible to please God. If you love God right, you are guaranteed to love everyone right. When you are joined to a living thing there is hope, a living dog is better than a dead lion. God will give you joy unspeakable, keep you in perfect peace when your mind is stayed on him; He will give you peace that surpasses all understanding.

Though I love my unsaved sisters, it is the saved woman who impresses me. All the curves, professional career with a large salary, and fashionable wardrobe is cool, but is secondary and doesn't mean anything if her inner man is messed up.

Jesus the Same Yesterday Today and Forevermore

The woman's physical shape does not mean anything without God. Everything may be tight right now, but eventually it is gonna start to sag. The material things are not the real you, the real you is what's on the inside. It's the heart, and as has already been mentioned, the heart is the soul and spirit or the emotions and mind of the person. The supernatural woman, God given, directed and instructed woman is who men should be searching for. According to the most recent research on New Year's resolutions, the top ten are:

1. Spend more time with family
2. Exercise more
3. Lose weight
4. Quit smoking
5. Enjoy life more (Less stress)
6. Quit drinking
7. Get out of debt
8. Learn something new
9. Help others
10. Get organized [42]

Jesus the Same Yesterday Today and Forevermore
While taking care of the outer man is vital, by comparison, the inner man is more important. What am I saying? Since the body carries out what the Lord instructs the inner man to do, it is important that the body be able to execute it. If your body is not in the shape to be able to carry it out, the work of the Lord goes lacking. It takes energy to be able to preach, and if the body is not up to deliver God's word, the will of God goes lacking.

Regarding the physical body, don't wait to take care of yourself, start today. I Corinthians 6:19 tells us that your body is the temple of the Holy Ghost. It's okay to have your grits, bacon, eggs, toasts, pancakes, fried potatoes, waffles, sausage, but do you have to eat it all at one meal? If you've been guilty just say ouch. I've always said eating is what I do best. I've been guilty of it myself, it's called over eating. If you are a child of God, your body is not your own, it belongs to God.

Some people partake in surgery to lose weight which is okay as long as they understand that they still have to deal

Jesus the Same Yesterday Today and Forevermore with the psychological aspect of losing weight. You still have to be disciplined, exercise, and eat properly. Which brings me back to the inner man; God wishes that we would prosper and be in good health even as our soul prospers, implying that good health comes from having a good soul. Could it be that people are in bad health because they are worn out mentally and emotionally? The most excellent way to go about changing your soul is to allow the Lord to change you.

When you accept Jesus Christ, old things are passed away, behold all things become new. God creates in you a clean heart and renews in you a right spirit. You become a new creature and your soul becomes converted, but if you never make the connection or understand the correlation between the soul and your mental state, you will never change.

Additional findings on New Year's resolutions are only twenty percent of those resolutions made in the month of January are successful and eighty percent are unsuccessful.

Jesus the Same Yesterday Today and Forevermore
Jesus declares for every natural situation there is a spiritual resolution that gives you the victory.

Throughout Bible history, the children of Israel put too much importance on ceremonial observations and God constantly incited them to do practical things that would make them better Christians. It is one thing to pray about a change, but if you don't get up off your knees and do what's right, your praying is in vain.

Paul instructs Christians in brotherly love, saying, how can you love God who you have never seen, and hate your brother who you see every day? He taught the people of God to practice entertaining and being hospitable to the stranger because he may be found to be a messenger of God for good. He further instructed the saints on keeping marriage sacred and that the duties of ministers are to be reverenced, respected and honored. This no doubt is what Christians of the past and present struggle to do. This is what provoked Paul to declare that Jesus is the same today, yesterday and forever more. It too is the reason why Paul

Jesus the Same Yesterday Today and Forevermore asked the Galatians, having begun in the spirit are you now made perfect in the flesh. You can make promises to change, but until you commit your ways unto the Lord, things will stay the same.

Jesus is our yesterday for all the mistreatment, lack of respect and being the black sheep of the family. In between yesterday and today is the night, the night symbolizes the suffering, but it is swallowed up by yesterday and today because Jesus is yesterday and today. Yesterday he hung and died on the cross for your sins. Today he is in glory at the right hand of the father making intercession for you and me. We cannot forget about our history, but we must live His-story.

Christ is your today and every day with him is a beautiful day. Today is the day that the Lord has made and you should rejoice and be glad in it. Tomorrow is Satan's today. He figures as long as he can get you to put God off until tomorrow, he's got you. Live life to the fullest, if you are single enjoy your singlehood, married enjoy your

Jesus the Same Yesterday Today and Forevermore marriage and if you are a teenager enjoy your youth, but most importantly live for the Lord today because your today determines your forever.

In order to get to your forever you must believe that Jesus is the same and act on this belief to do the future. To accomplish your forever you cannot give yourself to strange doctrines and false teachings. Let brotherly love continue and be not forgetful to entertain strangers. Remember them which have the rule over you, who have spoken unto you the word of God, but most importantly remember that Jesus is the same yesterday, today, and forevermore.

Chapter 21
Cut It Off

And it came to pass, when Jabin king of Hazor had heard those things, that he sent to Jobab, king of Madon, and to the king of Shimron, and to the king of Achshaph and to the kings that were on the north of the mountains, and of the plains south of Chinneroth, and in the valley, and in the borders of Dor on the west, and to the Canaanite on the east and on the west, and to the Amorite, and the Hittite, and the Perizzite, and the Jebusite in the mountains, and to the Hivite under Hermon in the land of Mizpeh. And they went out, they and all their hosts with them, much people, even as the sand that is upon the sea shore in multitude, with horses and chariots very many and when all these kings were met together, they came and pitched together at the waters of Merom, to fight against Israel and the Lord said unto Joshua, be not afraid because of them: for tomorrow about this time will I deliver them up all slain before Israel: thou shalt hock their horses, and burn their chariots with fire. So Joshua came, and all the people of war with him, against them by the waters of Merom suddenly; and they fell upon them and the Lord delivered them into the hand of Israel, who smote them, and chased them unto great Zidon, and unto Misrephothmaim and unto the valley of Mizpeh eastward; and they smote them, until they left them none remaining (Joshua 11:1-22).

It is not only a consecration of abilities that God wants, but of our inabilities also. An invalid was told that she could never escape from her prison of pain and weakness. "Oh well," she replied quickly, "there's a lot of living to be found within your limitations if you don't wear yourself out fighting them."
"Young lady," the doctor replied, "I wish I could have you preach to about a hundred of my patients a year." The lady was Helen Keller who said, "Face your deficiencies and acknowledge them, but do not let them master you."[20]

When you have the hope of God you're obedient, encouraging to others, sanctified, and you trust God, not man. You monitor your association with friends, organizations, and all relationships. You examine your connections, alliances, unions, and involvements. The word of God reminds us that we should not have a quarrelsome temper, and if thy hand offends thee, cut it off. It is better for you to enter into life maimed, than having two hands to go into hell, than into the fire that never shall be quenched. We should never have impure inclinations, and if thy right eye offends thee, pluck it out, and cast it from thee: for it is profitable for thee that one of thy members should perish, and not that thy whole body should be cast into hell. The aforementioned texts are not literal, but figuratively instructing the Christian to be peaceable and conciliatory.

Some people are always argumentative, confrontational and difficult, with contaminated ways, dirty habits, polluted behavior and poisonous conduct. These individuals are in danger of the Lord's judgment and hell's gates. It takes the hope of Christ to cut it off, but if they do, their life can become very significant, purposeful and significant. For example, the apostle Paul was blinded on the way to Damascus after having persecuted the saints of

God and participated in the stoning of Stephen. He heard from the Lord, implying that he listened to what the Lord had to say to him. The Bible says that the scales were removed from his eyes and straightway he began to preach, he didn't wait. All that heard Paul preach were amazed. He grabbed hold to the hope of Christ and started working for the Lord and the rest is history.

Rahab is another person who grabbed hold of the hope of Christ and began to live with purpose. Rahab, a harlot or prostitute, was a Canaanite of a cursed profession and people who heard about the power of Jesus. Despite the life style she was living, she is used of the Lord and becomes a believer. She heard the news of the miraculous deliverance from Egypt, placed her faith in the Lord, and was motivated into action. Her faith manifested itself as she hid the two spies in her own home. As a result, she was protected, delivered from destruction, married Salmon and became the ancestress of Boaz, David and Jesus. The result of cutting off destructive behavior and turning to righteous conduct doesn't get any better than this.

Cut It Off

Again, I will be the first to admit, sin can be pleasurable, been there done that, but it is pleasurable for a moment. Following the Lord is the key to cutting off sin. Total obedience brings about total victory. Joshua is a perfect example of what happens when you follow the Lord's instructions. A major figure in the events of the Exodus, he was charged with leading the people into battle. Identified as one of the twelve spies to explore the land of Canaan, he and Caleb gave an encouraging report. Some people can never be encouraging, but Joshua gave hope and confidence for which he was rewarded with entry into the Promised Land. He led the people across the Jordan River and showed leadership in the battle of Jericho.

Though Joshua followed the instructions of the Lord, he was defeated for the first time at Ai because of Achan. Immoral behavior can cause everything that you do to go wrong, and it can have negative implications for your entire family. Though Ai was defeated the second time, Achan's theft of the accursed thing from Jericho caused him and his family and his animals to be stoned to death. He like Adam and Eve brought guilt and disgrace on an entire nation because of his sin. The Lord instructs Joshua of Achan's behavior and tells him to deal with it. Joshua goes from heads of tribes to heads of family to the heads of households until he got to Achan and found that he stole an article of clothing. To this day Achan's grave site is called the valley of Achar which means trouble. If you don't defeat the enemy the first time he's coming around again. There is nothing worse than repeating destructive behavior with the same results, some would call that insanity.

Throughout Israel's history, God wanted them to trust in him and not in themselves or their military strength. In the aforementioned situation, he deliberately used a weak and small army to defeat Israelites, to show forth his power. God did not want the children of Israel to trust in the use of their horses and chariots, but to totally trust him. He tells them that their enemies would have horses and chariots and an army greater than theirs, but to fear not, even though they would be at a disadvantage.

Israel goes to battle to take the land of Canaan facing the kings of Northern Canaan which included an alliance with Hazor, ten times the size of Jerusalem. According to Josephus, the various Canaanite tribes totaled three hundred thousand infantry, ten thousand cavalry and twenty thousand war chariots. Joshua faced a force that was both numerically superior, technologically greater than his own, and it was the first time that Israel faced an enemy chariot corps. Due to their hope in God and following his instructions, the children of Israel were able to be victorious.

Hocking their horses meant cutting off the hamstring. Hamstring can be defined as the muscle that extends between the hip and knee joints or the bicep femor, semitendon and semimembrane. By severing these muscles, normal leg movement is disrupted, massive bleeding takes place, and the person becomes lame. This is what the Lord promised he would do for the children of Israel if they would just trust him. He did it for them and he wants to do it for you. The Lord will do the same for you if you cut off sin, unrighteous behavior and begin to trust him. Every place on which the sole of your foot treads the Lord will give to you, if you would take hold of his hope.

Chapter 22
Bewitched

O foolish Galatians, who hath bewitched you, that ye should not obey the truth, before whose eyes Jesus Christ hath been evidently set forth, crucified among you? This only would I learn of you, received ye the Spirit by the works of the law, or by the hearing of faith? Are ye so foolish? Having begun in the Spirit, are ye now made perfect by the flesh? (Galatians 3:1-3).

Great Britain's Pagan Federation, which represents witches, claimed that the TV shows *Buffy the Vampire Slayer* and *Sabrina the Teenage Witch*, fueled a rapidly growing interest in witchcraft among children. The organization averaged one hundred inquiries a month from kids who wanted to become witches, during which time it appointed its first ever youth officer to counsel young people.[44]

At my first dorm meeting in Perry Hall at Lincoln University, my freshmen dorm director, a small man in stature, stood on a chair with three fingers and his thumb pointed at us, and asked the question "Why are you here?" This happened over thirty six years ago and I've never forgotten it. What he wanted us to do was examine ourselves, something I try to on a daily basis to make sure I am still in the faith. This examination is necessary to maintain your salvation, have persistent deliverance, manage your marriage and family, and love your neighbor.

As a preacher of the gospel of Jesus Christ, I understand that people come to church for many different reasons, but the Christian should constantly want the Lord to create in them a clean heart and renew in them a right spirit. The follower of Christ desires to be lead by the spirit because he is interested in the word of God falling on good ground and learning how to live peaceably amongst all men. The Christian's greatest aspiration is not forty inch rims on an SUV, but becoming bold as a lion, confident in the Lord, walking in the spirit and not fulfilling the lust of the flesh. Thereby, they are able to love their family and fellowman.

Bewitched

There is something to be said about the true Christian, the one who is lead by the spirit, studies God's word, prays for all people, and is a good witness for the Lord.

The aforementioned believer has self control, the type of peace that sweeps the soul, builds up the body of Christ and does not sow discord amongst the brethren. This individual sees the big picture, believes that Jesus went away to prepare a place for them. They further believe that in their father's house is many mansions, and they want to hear God say enter in, well done thou good and faithful servant.

The Christian, who regularly asks what can separate him from the love of God, is a person who desires accountability, does not want to hurt others, and wants love to flow from their heart freely. Loving others and spreading joy becomes difficult only when we try to do it on our own. True adoration and happiness was bought with a price. It cannot be purchased from man, but can only come from God. This person has made up their mind to serve the Lord, be committed to faithfulness, and will not allow themselves to be bewitched.

Before you get on the Galatians, ask yourself, when was the last time you were bewitched. Bewitched can be defined as to influence or affect especially injuriously by witchcraft, to attract by witchcraft or cast a spell. Witchcraft can also be defined as communicating with the devil. You may be saying, I don't communicate with Satan, but we have to be extra careful that our behavior is not as such. If a person thinks, act, or behaves in a hateful fashion, and believes they are not being influence by Satan, they are being bewitched.

People are being bewitched by a lot of different things on a daily basis. Drugs, the love of money, houses, good looking men and the cookie, are all things that are deceiving people. Y'all know what the cookie is right? The cookie has no respect of person and a man can crumble under its control, just ask former New York Governor Elliot Spitzer, former South Carolina Governor

Mark Sanford and President Bill Clinton. Even preachers can be bewitched by the cookie, just ask Jimmy Swaggart and Bishop Eddie Long. Just when you think you have cornered the market on holiness here comes Satan.

In your daily assessment of yourself, you should always remember that all have sinned and fallen short of the glory of God and for the wages of sin is death, but the gift of God is eternal life through Jesus Christ our Lord. God wishes that none would perish, but that all would come to repentance. So, we should always show mercy toward people.

God told Eve that she would die if she ate from the tree of good and evil, but he told Adam first. When Satan told Eve she would be as a God knowing good and evil, she allowed herself to be bewitched. This implies that we allow ourselves to be deceived because of what we want. It can be argued that Adam and Eve wanted to be a know it all which was Satan's attitude in the beginning. In the book of Isaiah, the Bible reveals that Satan said he would be like the most high. Having the status of Chief Cherub wasn't good enough for him. Satan is a deceiver, the arch deceiver, who presents himself as light by dressing himself up as something good.

Sometimes people can bewitch you, Saul is an example. God made him king of Israel and instead of following the voice of the Lord, he listened to the voice of the people. It's okay to listen to those who do not know the Lord, but concerning spiritual things, we should always listen to God. God takes the mantle from Saul who he used for his glory and passes it to David. This means that God reserves the right to use you and refuse you. David is anointed king of Israel only to be bewitched by a woman.

Paul tells the people of God that Christ was crucified among them, but their disobedience was evidence that they were being bewitched. He reminds them of how close they were to Jesus and how they observed him be crucified. Seeing Christ crucified should have been enough to counteract all fascination with legalism. A people who were naturally sharp, had lost their ability to reason and common sense. Paul asked, what caused you to be misled and then reproves them for abandoning the faith. He exhorts that salvation is by faith and not the law.

While the law lets us know when we are in violation, separated from God, and not following him, the spirit teaches us the word, leads us into all truth, and convicts us when we do wrong. Some people have been bewitched for so long that they don't know the truth from a lie. Satan wants to strip you and leave you naked and ashamed, the consequences of being bewitched. Paul reminds us that faith comes by hearing and hearing by the word of God, we wrestle not against flesh and blood, but against principalities in high places, and by taking on the whole armor of God we defend ourselves from being bewitched. For those of you who have no desire to live a righteous life, you should know that Satan desires to strip you and leave you naked and ashamed.

Bewitched

When asked where his brother was, Cain who was bewitched into killing Able, ask Jesus if he was his brother's keeper. He answered God in a very condescending way, suggesting, don't you know where he is, you're God. Knowing what Cain had done, God was giving him an opportunity to repent. Peter who denied Christ repented and God commissioned him to strengthen the brethren. No matter what we have done in the past God still loves us, but he hates the sin. Give your life to the Lord today and allow him to take you to great heights.

Chapter 23
Temptation a Promise

There hath no temptation taken you but such as is common to man, but God is faithful, who will not suffer you to be tempted above that ye are able, but will with the temptation also make a way to escape, that ye may be able to bear it (I Corinthians 10:13).

In the Australian bush country grows a little plant called the sundew. It has a slender stem and tiny round leaves fringed with hairs that glisten with bright drops of liquid as delicate as fine dew. But woe to the insect, that dares to dance on it. Although its attractive clusters of red, white, and pink blossoms are harmless, the leaves are deadly. The shiny moisture on each leaf is sticky and will imprison any bug that touches it. As an insect struggles to free itself, the vibration causes the leaves to close tightly around it. This innocent looking plant then feeds on its victim.[38] The sundew plant grows in soil that lacks important minerals, especially nitrogen. Therefore, special organs enable the

Temptation a Promise

sundew plant to digest the insects' body which provides the minerals that it needs to survive.

We are living in the end times, a period before Jesus is to return. Timothy tells us that in the last days perilous times shall come. Perilous times according to the Bible are defined as men being lovers of their own selves, loving to gratify their own lust, and having no Christian charity. It is a dangerous period when men are boasters, proud, unthankful, unholy, and lovers of pleasure more than lovers of God.

Though one may fall into diver's temptation, temptation in and of itself is not a sin. If it were sin, James never would have advised Christians to count it all joy when you fall into diver's temptation. Temptation is not all bad or good, but neither is it a license to sin. James was dealing with people who were sick and afflicted, persecuted, mistreated, and threatened. He taught to be joyful during temptation because it teaches patience, love, kindness and helps you to work out your own soul salvation. When Satan

Temptation a Promise attempts to lure, pull, and entice you to sin, it is an opportunity to add to your testimony and develop Christian character. Though some Christians don't want to be tested, it's a promise in this the dispensation of grace, the period when free moral agents are tested.

Paul advised Timothy to warn his people that the seducer prays on the weak, those who don't have the ability to defend themselves due to a lack of prayer, bible study and poor church attendance. Many people are enticed to mistreat, injure and murder others because they do not practice Hebrews 10:25 "Forsake not the assembling of ourselves together." You cannot call yourself a Christian or a follower of Christ and not have regular church attendance. The house of the Lord is where you find peace, strength, understanding, and fellowship. It is the place where you are taught how to defend yourself.

When you accept Christ, old things are passed away, behold all things become new. There has to be a change in heart. The book of Romans informs us that we should be

Temptation a Promise

transformed by the renewing of our mind. When you adopt God's way of thinking, your thoughts become good thoughts; you have a change of attitude and not just a form of Godliness. You don't want to be the type of Christian, who looks, sounds, and shouts like you're Godly, but Satan is walking your dog every day. Anybody can praise God, but those that worship him must worship him in spirit and in truth. The drunkard, dope dealer, and promiscuous person can praise him, but only the true Christian can be lead by the spirit.

God is not disappointed or displeased when we are tempted. The book of Genesis records God's temptation of Abraham which at the surface appears to be in conflict with James' proclamation that God tempts no man. Abraham welcomed the temptation to sacrifice his son to prove his faithfulness to the Lord. Jesus when tempted by Satan declared that man must not live by bread alone, but by every word that proceeds out of the mouth of God. He further declared that it is written thou shall not tempt the Lord God, and thou shalt worship the Lord thy God and

Temptation a Promise

him only shalt thou serve. Stephen started out as a deacon, became a powerful preacher, and ended up being a martyr for the faith. Nelson Mandela fought against apartheid and civil injustice and in the end was victorious. Abraham, Jesus, Stephen and Mandela are all examples of being tempted and passing the test.

Christians must understand that we are dealing with a two thousand year old devil, and be sober and vigilant because our adversary, the devil, who as a roaring lion, walketh about, seeking whom he may devour. Satan said he would return into his house from whence he came, wanting to find it empty, swept, and garnished. God saves delivers and sets us free, but if we don't maintain our spiritual being the devil can possess us again. Some of the things we are getting involved in can't be blamed on the devil. For example, if you are a single Christian you can't invite a man or woman over for a candle light dinner, and think nothing is going to happen. The next thing you know you are in the bed with the person violating God's word by becoming a fornicator.

Temptation a Promise

Don't let a man or woman, boyfriend or girlfriend, separate you from the love of God. Cain sold his birth right for a bowl of porridge, Eve was deceived by the serpent, and Adam simply gave into sin. Blessed is the man that endures temptation, for when he is tried he shall receive a crown of life. God cannot be tempted with evil neither tempteth he any man, but every man is tempted when he is drawn away of his own lust. Lust when it is conceived brings forth sin and sin death. Sin is defined as that which is not faith, transgression of the law, and all unrighteousness. If you are living a lifestyle that is in conflict with the life of Christ and think you were born that way, you must be born again. Nicodemus said how can a man be reborn when he is old not realizing it was a spiritual thing.

Some believe that spiritual maturity will exempt them from being harassed by temptation, but enticement will be a part of this earth until Jesus returns. A recent survey taken by *Discipleship Journal* readers ranked areas of

Temptation a Promise

greatest spiritual challenge to them. Materialism, pride, self centeredness, laziness, and sexual lust ranked very high. Temptations were more potent when readers neglected their time with God (eighty-one percent) and were physically tired (fifty-one). Resisting temptation was accomplished by prayer (eighty-four percent), avoiding compromising situations (seventy-six percent), Bible study (sixty-six percent), and being accountable to someone (fifty-two percent).[40]

Corinth was a place where sexual sin and lust was at an all time high. It was actually reported that there was sexual immorality among them and of a kind that did not occur even among pagans; a man had his father's wife. Paul advised the Corinthians to resist the spirit of Corinth and not allow it to overtake them. As Paul reminded the Corinthian church to resist temptation, we too should remember that fornicators, idolaters, adulterers, effeminates, and abusers of self shall not inherit the kingdom of God. Paul further stated, "I discipline my body and bring it into subjection, lest, when I have preached to others, I myself should not see heaven."

There hath no temptation taken you but such as is common to man, but God is faithful, who will not suffer you to be tempted above that ye are able, but will with the temptation also make a way to escape, that ye may be able to bear it. He may not take the temptation away and it may be frequent and regular, but you can bear it if you understand when God is challenging you and when Satan is tempting you. God promises that we will be tried and can come out as pure gold. Temptation is designed to take us through the fire to get rid of the impurities, defects, and test our genuineness for God.

Chapter 24
Judgment Day

It is appointed unto men once to die, but after this the judgment. Christ was once offered to bear the sins of many and unto them that look for him shall he appear the second time without sin unto salvation (Hebrews 9:27-28).

When I stand at the Judgment Seat of Christ and he shows me his plan for me, the plan of my life as it might have been had he had his way, and I see how I blocked him here and I checked him there and I would not yield my will, shall I see grief in my Savior's eyes, grief though he loves me still? Oh, he'd have me rich, and I stand there poor, stripped of all but his grace, while my memory runs like a hunted thing down paths I can't retrace. Then my desolate heart will nearly break with tears that I cannot shed. I'll cover my face with my empty hands and bow my uncrowned head. Lord, of the years that are left to me I yield them to thy hand. Take me, make me, and mold me to the pattern thou hast planned. For I understand that the

Judgment Day

Judgment Seat is meant for the professing Christians, real and imperfect Christians.[47]

How many of you know that we have to be ready when we die, ready for the afterlife. If you are physically and spiritually alive when the trumpet sounds you will be caught up to meet Christ in the air. If you are physically dead, but spiritually alive when the trumpet sounds, you also will be caught up. The difference is if you are physically and spiritually alive when the trumpet sounds, you will not experience physical death until the rapture takes place. But, if you are already physically dead, you're already spiritually present with the Lord at the sounding of the trumpet. The Bible declares that we shall be changed in a moment, in a twinkling of an eye. Judgment day is about both death and life. You can't preach on one without mentioning the other, people fall under one or the other.

The thief comes to steal, kill and destroy, but Jesus came to give life. There is a sin unto death and that sin is simply

Judgment Day

not accepting Jesus Christ as Lord and savior. Only living spirits are going to be in heaven. There won't be any dead spirits there. For the sinner hell is a bottomless pit, no physical solid surroundings, and total isolation. Utter darkness, a person is isolated, restricted, and forever to him or herself.

Sometimes it seems no matter what you say to unsaved people about God it isn't good enough. You can say God is a deliverer, miracle worker, and savior who can change their life and living situations and it is as if it doesn't matter to them. I am thoroughly convinced that people feel and act this way because sin is pleasurable. My hope and prayer is that more of my family and friends would prepare themselves for the life to come with the attitude Moses once had. Moses suffered affliction with the people of God, rather than enjoy the pleasures of sin for a season. What we as Christians have to understand is that the world's pleasure is for a season and so is the affliction of the righteous, but the pleasures of the righteous are for an eternity. We must look to the hills from which comes our help and ask our self, what shall it profit a man to gain the whole world and lose his soul?

During his time on earth Paul cajoled the people of God to continue to strive for God's goodness and not revert back to their old belief system. He was trying to get them to understand that Christ offered himself to God, cleansed their consciences from acts that lead to death, so that they could serve the living God. This is a constant battle for all Christians, but if we allow Christ to be our mediator, mind regulator and perfect peace, we will not deteriorate, relapse or return to our old ways.

Life with Jesus is much better than it is without the king of kings and Lord of lords. Don't go back to fornication, smoking marijuana, being a drunk or a whore monger. God's people wanted to return to a place where they would be governed by the first covenant, a place where the conscience was not purged, sins were not put away, and entrance into the holiest was not granted to the worshipers. Jesus cleared the way and allows us to cast our cares on him because he cares for us. We can now get to the father through him and have no need for anyone else.

Through Christ we now have an opened way into the sanctuary of God. Purification of the conscience and eternal redemption comes through Jesus. Christ's sacrifice allows us to make daily intercession with him and he appears in the presence of God for us. He presents our person and performances to God, rebukes our adversary and accuser, secures our interest and has prepared a mansion for each and every one of us. Who wouldn't want to serve someone like this?

Our days are numbered on this earth, the millennial period is on its way, and soon there will be a new heaven and earth. There are seven dispensations of man and they are innocence, conscience, human government, promise, law, grace, and the millennial period. The periods of innocence and conscience primarily involved Adam and Eve's fall from grace. Human government was a period when Noah and his family repopulated the earth after the flood.

Judgment Day

Abraham was the promise, Moses represents the law, we are currently in the dispensation of grace represented by the crucifixion of Christ and the millennial period is the period to come when Christ and the Christians will rule for a thousand years.

What I call the spiritual calendar looks like this. The next significant event is the rapture when the dead in Christ shall be raised first, then those who are alive and remain shall be caught up to meet him in the air. Alive and remain means spiritually transformed not simply having breath. Immediately once the rapture takes place, the tribulation period will begin, a period of seven years where there will be death and destruction, followed by the second coming of Christ and the battle of Armageddon. The millennial period comes after the day of reckoning and will last a thousand years, followed by the final judgment and new heaven and earth.

So, what does Paul mean when he says it is appointed to all men to die and then the judgment? We all are going to

Judgment Day

die physically, but to be absent in the body is to be present with the Lord. Paul is asking will you spend an eternity in heaven with the Lord or in hell with Satan. If you accept Jesus Christ as your lord and savior you will spend an eternity with him. If you have not accepted Christ you are already spiritually dead, will spend an eternity in hell with Satan, but you can alter your course with rebirth. You can do that right now in about fifteen seconds by simply saying, "Dear Lord, I am a sinner, forgive me of my sin, come into my life, I want to live for you, thank you." If you prayed that simple prayer you can consider yourself a born again Christian. Judgment day just got easier for you. You are now entitled to the Bema Seat or Judgment Seat of Christ, the rapture or to be present with the Lord upon physical death. This for the Godly causes joy, hope is no longer deferred, the desire has come and it is a tree of life, but to not know the Lord in the parting of your sins will bring terror to you.

As a true believer you can by faith look with hope for the return of Christ. Through your holy desires, duty, ordinance and providence, honestly anticipate the second coming and prepare for it. And though it will be a sudden destruction to the rest of the world, who mock at the report of it, it will be eternal salvation to those of us who look for it.

Chapter 25
Can You Take It

Therefore being justified by faith, we have peace with God through our Lord Jesus Christ, by whom also we have access by faith into this grace wherein we stand, and rejoice in hope of the glory of God. And not only so, but we glory in tribulations also, knowing that tribulation worketh patience, and patience, experience and experience, hope. And hope maketh not ashamed, because the love of God is shed abroad in our hearts by the Holy Ghost which is given unto us. For when we were yet without strength, in due time Christ died for the ungodly. For scarcely for a righteous man will one die, yet peradventure for a good man some would even dare to die. But God commended his love toward us, in that, while we were yet sinners, Christ died for us (Romans 5:1-8).

Authorities investigated the wife and son of an Illinois police officer who allegedly killed himself after embezzling money for years from a youth police explorer program he oversaw. Investigators said they believed the

Can You Take It

thirty year police veteran whose death prompted a long manhunt and whose funeral drew thousands of mourners, killed himself because his criminal activity was about to be exposed. Up until the day he was found dead, a new village administrator was pressing him to see the explorer program's books as part of a village wide audit. "It's breaking my heart," said a local forty-one year old school bus mechanic. "There is a 'We love you, Joe' sign that I pass by every day. And now it has been taken down." Lake County Major Crimes Task Force Commander George Filenko said text messages and other records showed the police officer embezzled from the village's police explorer program for seven years, spending the money on mortgage payments, travel expenses, gym memberships, adult websites and loans to friends.[3]

Hope in Christ gives us the ability to endure many situations and circumstances, not give up and hang tough in this journey called life. We are reminded by Ecclesiastes that the race is not given to the swift nor to the strong, but to the one who endures to the end. To endure is to have fortitude, stamina and strength. How does a person gain endurance? The book of Romans says suffering produces endurance. So, before you can have fortitude, stamina, and strength, it helps to have suffered for Christ. Some of us have not suffered, are weak spiritually, and as a result, can't take anything.

A weak person is someone who is always crying about something. One thing the Lord has blessed me with is endurance. I consider myself to be someone who can take some stuff without crying the blues. I'm not saying that you should take someone abusing you in any kind of way, but God gives us a strong backbone. As for me and my house, I will serve the Lord.

I will use myself as an example. I am the head elder at Integrity Deliverance Church, a professor, probation officer, and the parent of two wonderful young adults. Let me begin with divorce; who wants to go through a divorce? Raise your hand. While going through the divorce, I got accused of having an affair with another leader in Integrity. The lie was told to defame me and was used as an excuse to get out of the marriage. This was done after seventeen years of being faithful to my wife, helping her create two successful businesses, and being prophet, priest and king of my home. Couple that with the fact that I have been passed over for promotion several times, by people who are less educated and have less experience. One individual was in grade school when I started working for the probation department and the other was in junior high school. The youngest individual I actually taught in the classroom at Heartland Community College. The book of Romans calls that suffering. Some of us haven't suffered anything so it's difficult to take anything.

The book of Romans further implies that when you suffer you develop Christ like character. Character is who you are, your qualities, temperament, personality. Personality is the sum of your character traits and individual behavior. I start each semester at Heartland Community College by asking each student to tell the class one good quality about him/her. This is something that Christian people should not struggle with. And it doesn't matter how many times you've made an honest mistake, you always have an advocate with the father.

To understand the type of character we should have, look no further than Matthew 6:33 where it says seek ye first the kingdom of God and his righteousness, and all these things will be added to you. The things are the needs that you have, and his righteousness is synonymous with Christ's personality traits, those traits that sum up Jesus. All the traits Paul was trying to get the people of God to practice: faith, to glory not in men, forgiving, take no stock in the world, serve God and make yourself second to God.

To gain the character of Christ you have to suffer. Look at all that Christ suffered, which included being crucified on the cross. His suffering produced endurance and endurance produced character and character produced hope. Hope is anticipation, expectation and what you look forward to.

When Timothy proclaims to suffer with him is to reign with him, he means to suffer is to endure. To endure builds character and building character gives you hope, including the ultimate hope that you will reign with him. We learned from chapter one that hope deferred maketh the heart sick. If something is deferred it is late, not on time, postponed, or tardy. Sick means bad, ill, unwell, but remember to him that is joined to all the living there is hope and a living dog is better than a dead lion.

A person, who can take it, does not destroy self or others, or commit suicide or murder. Remember you are God's child, the salt of the earth, a peculiar person, the light of the world, like a light that sits upon a hill that cannot be hid, but can you take it? The person who committed suicide suffered not for Christ's sake, but was unwilling to give his life to God and grab a hold of the hope that would have delivered him from the ill feelings, attitude and belief that took him to his grave.

Can You Take It

I'm saying to you today that you can make it, but you have to fight. Since I've been on planet earth there have been some iconic boxing matches at the heavyweight division. None more dramatic than the Mike Tyson and Michael Spinks fight. Spinks at the time was thirty-one and zero and Mike Tyson was thirty-four and zero. Tyson knocked Spinks out in one minute and thirty-three seconds. George Forman v. Muhammad Ali and Sony Liston v. Ali were two classic boxing matches, but no fight was greater than the Thriller in Manila. Ali and Frazier had very contrasting styles, approaches and strategies and over the years fought a total of forty-one rounds with neither giving an inch and both giving their all. At seeming the edge of death Frazer didn't answer the bell for round fifteen and Ali said, prior to his passing; it was the closest he had ever come to death. We all have different styles, approaches and strategies but we use the word of God to fight for our life.

The book of Romans says to present your body a living sacrifice, holy and acceptable to God. As you put up a good fight, what you can't do is get weary in well doing. Galatians says "Be not weary in well doing for in due season you will reap if you faint not." Let us do well to all men whether they are in the house of faith or not a part of God's kingdom. If you don't give in and give up, you are going to experience joy and peace.

To know what to do when you get tired, look no further than the gospel of Mark who depicts Jesus as the tireless servant. Jesus never got tired of serving God, sacrificed his life, and then told God not to hold it against his murderers because they knew not what they did. No man took his life, but he laid it down that we might have life and life more abundantly. We have to allow the Lord to fight our battle, it is not ours anyway.

Jesus served in many ways; he dwelled among humanity as a man, obeyed God's will, ministered to the disciples and ultimately died on the cross. I don't know about you, but I want to see Jesus in the end and to do that, I have to endure and be able to suffer some things. What a great day it is going to be when we see Jesus, the man that died for you and me, set us free, and gave his life for us. We will then experience the fullness of joy, heavenly joy, and no greater joy. Greater joy hath no man than this that a man lay down his life for a friend. You are a friend of the king of kings and lord of lords and you too can take it.

Chapter 26

Standing in the Gap

When the Son of Man shall come in his glory, and all the holy angels with him, then shall he sit upon the throne of his glory: And before him shall be gathered all nations and he shall separate them one from another, as a shepherd divides his sheep from the goat. And he shall set the sheep on his right hand, but the goats on the left. Then shall the king say unto them on his right hand, come, ye blessed of my Father, inherit the kingdom prepared for you from the foundation of the world. For I was a hungered, and ye gave me meat, I was thirsty, and ye gave me drink, I was a stranger, and ye took me in, naked, and ye clothed me, I was sick, and ye visited me, I was in prison, and ye came unto me (Matthew 25:31-46).

Then shall the righteous answer him, saying, Lord, when saw we thee a hungered, and fed thee? Or thirsty, and gave thee drink? When saw we thee a stranger, and took thee in? Or naked, and clothed thee? Or when saw we thee sick, or in prison, and came unto thee? And the king shall

Standing in the Gap

answer and say unto them, Verily I say unto you, inasmuch as ye have done it unto one of the least of these my brethren, ye have done it unto me. Then shall he say also unto them on the left hand, depart from me, ye cursed, into everlasting fire, prepared for the devil and his angels: For I was an hungered, and ye gave me no meat, I was thirsty, and ye gave me no drink, I was a stranger, and ye took me not in, naked and ye clothed me not, sick and in prison, and ye visited me not. Then shall they also answer him, saying, Lord, when saw we thee a hungered, or a thirst, or a stranger, or naked, or sick, or in prison, and did not minister unto thee? Then shall he answer them, saying, verily I say unto you, inasmuch as ye did it not to one of the least of these, ye did it not to me. And these shall go away into everlasting punishment, but the righteous into life eternal (Matthew 25:37-46).

Auto maker Henry Ford was vacationing in Ireland when he was asked to contribute toward a new orphanage. Ford wrote a check for two thousand pounds which made headlines in the local newspaper. But the paper inadvertently reported the gift as twenty thousand pounds. The director of the orphanage apologized to Ford, "I'll phone the editor right away and tell him to correct the mistake," he said. "There's no need for that," Ford replied, and promptly wrote a check for the additional eighteen thousand pounds.[35]

Standing in the gap means praying for the Christian person and for the individual who doesn't know the Lord. The Bible declares where two or three are gathered in his name he shall be in the midst and the fervent effectual prayer of the righteous avails much.

Standing in the gap means that as a Christian you are on your post even when the pastor is out of town. Standing in the gap means that you can fellowship with anyone who is lifting up the name of Jesus, no matter what their race or ethnicity.

Some people have their favorite preachers, teachers and pastors and will listen to them only. The Bible says rejoice with those who do rejoice. If you want people to rejoice when you rejoice, you should not find it difficult to worship and praise God with others. Each and every one of us is different and though we may worship differently, if Jesus is the center of the praise and worship, we should be able to respond in a Christian like way.

A good leadership quality is to lead by example. In other words, if you want people to get behind you, you get behind, encourage, and build up others. When your pastor is out of town, all hands should be on deck. That is not the time to go on your personal mission trip; you have a job to do.

The reason you can't go on your personal mission trip in the pastor's absence is because the word of God has to be preached, someone has to teach Sunday school, ushers have to usher, Deacons have a responsibility, someone has to work the alter, and an offering has to be received. I'll put it this way; you still have to have church.

When a Christian prejudicially decides who he can spiritually listen to, he is in danger of falling away from the faith and can end up in a place of apostasy. The apostle Paul encourages us to not be a respecter of person, but to be our brother's keeper. He said let us consider how we may spur one another on toward love and good deeds. Paul further said let us encourage one another the more as we see the day approaching.

You can't help your brother, or anyone else, if you are in a state of apostasy or falling away from the faith. If you have to always be concerned about you, there is little to no time for you to minister to others. The book of Hebrews teaches that our mind should be attentively fixed on each other to render mutual help and counsel.

The Son of Man has come; he has been placed on his throne of grace, and judgment is taking place. Every man shall be sentenced to a state of everlasting happiness or misery based on what he does in this world of trial and probation. The administration of Judgment on that great day is committed to the Lord. The appearing of all the children of men before Christ will be to determine who stood in the gap for others.

The distinction that will then be made between the Christian and those who refused to follow Christ will be separated one from another, as the tares and wheat are separated at the harvest, and the good fish and the bad at the shore. Just as the wicked and godly dwell together in the same homes, they dwell together in the same cities, churches, families, and are not certainly distinguishable one from another. The godly are like sheep, innocent, mild, patient, useful and the wicked are like goats, unsavory, nasty, unpleasant and unruly. The sheep and goats are feeding all day in the same pasture, but he will set the saved on his right hand and the unsaved on his left. To the unsaved he will say when I was hungry you fed me not, when I was thirsty you gave me nothing to drink, when I was clothed less you gave me nothing to wear, and when I was homeless you didn't give me shelter.

Standing in the Gap

The unsaved will not realize it until it is too late; they imagined it was only poor, weak, and silly people who made more to do than needed about religion. They will not comprehend that when they did it against the least of Christ's followers, he would take as done against himself. It will be like putting a millstone around their neck and throwing themselves into the deep part of the sea.

Christians who make it to heaven will wonder why God so regarded them and their services. It is not that the saints won't believe they belong in heaven, but they will be humbled to find such poor and worthless services, as theirs, be so highly celebrated, and richly rewarded. Christ will show his mighty regard to works of charity and how he is especially pleased with kindness done to his people for his sake. The good works of the Christians, when they are produced in the great day shall all be remembered; not even a cup of water given shall be overlooked. Hang in there, you can take it, stand in the gap and watch how the Lord will reward you here on earth and in heaven.

Chapter 27
The Death Penalty

But the rest of the dead lived not again until the thousand years were finished. This is the first resurrection. Blessed and holy is he that hath part in the first resurrection: on such the second death hath no power, but they shall be priests of God and of Christ, and shall reign with him a thousand years. And when the thousand years are expired, Satan shall be loosed out of his prison, and shall go out to deceive the nations which are in the four quarters of the earth, Gog and Magog, to gather them together to battle, the number of whom is as the sand of the sea. And they went up on the breadth of the earth, and compassed the camp of the saints about, and the beloved city, and fire came down from God out of heaven, and devoured them. And the devil that deceived them was cast into the lake of fire and brimstone, where the beast and the false prophet are, and shall be tormented day and night for ever and ever. And I saw a great white throne, and him that sat on it, from whose face the earth and the heaven fled away, and there was found no place for them. And I saw the

The Death Penalty

dead, small and great, stand before God, and the books were opened, and another book was opened, which is the book of life, and the dead were judged out of those things which were written in the books, according to their works. And the sea gave up the dead, who were in it, and death and hell delivered up the dead who were in them, and they were judged every man according to their works. And death and hell were cast into the lake of fire. This is the second death. And whosoever was not found written in the book of life was cast into the lake of fire (Revelations 20:5-15).

A Christian railroad engineer was speaking to a group of fellow workers about heaven. He said, "I can't begin to tell you what the Lord Jesus means to me. In him I have a hope that is very precious. Let me explain. Many years ago as each night I neared the end of my run, I would always let out a long blast with the whistle just as I'd come around the last curve. Then I'd look up at the familiar little cottage on top of the hill. My mother and father would be standing in the doorway waving to me. After I had passed, they'd go

The Death Penalty

back inside and say, thank God, Benny is home safe again tonight. Well, they are gone now, and no one is there to welcome me. But someday when I have finished my earthly run and I draw near to heaven's gate, I believe I'll see my precious mother and dad waiting there for me. And the one will turn to the other and say, thank God, Benny is home safe at last."[22]

Chapter twelve of this book, *These Three Words*, emphasizes the importance of expressing love for your family and fellow man, being able to say the words, I Love You. I asked you when was the last time you told someone that you love them. You were reminded that tomorrow is not promised, that you should tell family, friends, and even enemies that you love them because life is too short to hate people. These Three Words proclaims that you should love your neighbor as you love yourself and love yourself more than you probably do. Remember, the word of God teaches that you can't say you love God who you have never seen and hate your brother who you see every day.

The Death Penalty

In addition to Christ, Boaz and Ruth were used to emphasize what love really is. The subject of this chapter may seem to be just the opposite of These Three Words, but God's word is quick, and powerful, and sharper than any two edged sword, piercing even to the dividing asunder of the soul and spirit, and of the joints and marrow. The word of God too is a discerner of the thoughts and intents of the heart. My prayer is for you to understand that these are the last days and you're living to live again. You should be positive in all situations, desire that your heart be fortified for success, and pray that the Lord does not take his spirit from you.

God wishes that none would perish and that all would come to repentance. Hell was made for Satan and his angels, not for me and you. It was Satan that said I will ascend to the top of the clouds, I will be like the most high, and I will be god.

Remember David the son of Jesse, a man after God's own heart, did a whole lot of dirt prior to having Uriah killed.

The Death Penalty

He committed the sins of fornication, adultery and murder. Fornication in the Illinois Criminal Code is a class B misdemeanor punishable by up to one hundred and eighty days in jail. It is defined as an offense committed when one person has sexual intercourse with another who is not their spouse. Adultery in the Illinois Statute is a class A misdemeanor punishable by up to three hundred and sixty five days in jail. It is defined as a person who has sexual intercourse with another who is not this/her spouse and one of the people involved in the sexual intercourse must be married, and the defendant must have knowledge of this fact.

You may wonder why people are not regularly charged with the aforementioned law violations. Well, the statute says that it has to be done in an open and notorious way. In other words, the police are not going to come to your house and arrest you for fornication and adultery.

David understood that there was a plan of salvation, and that he could repent of his sins. He knew that if he

The Death Penalty

acknowledged his sin, asked forgiveness, and then committed his life to God, he would be okay. That is why the Lord said he was a man after his own heart, not because of the sin, but because he had sense enough to ask for forgiveness.

So it stands to reason that God doesn't care what you have done in your past, he doesn't care how much dirt you have done, he throws your sin into the sea of forgetfulness, washes you and makes you whiter than snow. Old things are passed away, behold all things have become new.

It is appointed to all men to die and then the judgment. David knew his days were numbered, so he lived like there was no tomorrow. Sometimes I find myself asking where all the days went. We are living on God's mercy, tomorrow is not promised and you can die before your time.

There was a period in time when man was subject to the Code of Hammurabi, named after the sixth king of

The Death Penalty

Babylon, who ruled for forty two years, and ruled under an eye for an eye. Hammurabi codified the death penalty for twenty-five different crimes. As we got closer to Jesus' birth it got worse with people receiving death sentences by means of crucifixion, drowning, beating, burning and impalement. A person who was killed by impalement was killed by stake, spear, and hook.

Remember, there is a sin unto death which is why the Bible teaches us to examine ourselves daily to make sure we are found in the faith. If anyone sees his brother commit a sin that does not lead to death, he should pray and God will give him life. Jesus hung on the cross, but no sin did he commit. Stephen was stoned to death for preaching the word of God, but no sin did he commit. Therefore, we must conclude that John is referring to spiritual death.

Another way of putting it is there is a sin that can lead to spiritual death. The book of Romans posits that all have sinned and fallen short of the glory of God, the wages of

The Death Penalty

sin are death, and this includes Christians who have sinned and individuals who have never repented of their sins. A Christian can sin in such a way that will bring him back into spiritual death and endanger him to the lake of fire again.

Now the works of the flesh are manifest, which are these: adultery, fornication, uncleanness, lasciviousness, idolatry, witchcraft, hatred, variance, emulations, wrath, strife, seditions, heresies, envyings, murders, drunkenness, revelings, and such like; of the which I tell you before, as I have also told you in times past, that they which do such things shall not inherit the kingdom of God, the spiritual death penalty (Galatians 5:19-21).

John, the author of Revelations, lets us know that he saw an angel with a chain and key come from heaven, lay hold on Satan, also known as the dragon and the devil, and cast him into a bottomless pit. John further saw those that were beheaded for the gospel,

The Death Penalty

martyrs, and witnesses for the gospel. He saw the first resurrection, those caught up to meet Jesus in the air, and judgment day. Judgment day consists of the world, dead, young and old, low and high, rich and poor and the righteous being judged, known as that great day.

For those of us who will be at the Bema Seat of Christ this is just formality, conformation, as our portion will have been fixed long before judgment day. We will be in the Lamb's Book of Life and serve as assistants to Christ.

The death penalty will be for the sinner who refused to give his life to Christ and the Christian in a backslidden state who failed to repent. I hope you do not want to be a part of the second resurrection when death and hell will be turned over into the lake of fire.

Chapter 28
Have You Heard

A young minister in a college town was embarrassed by the thought of criticism in his cultured congregation. He sought counsel from his father, an old and wise minister, saying, "Father, I am hampered in my ministry in the pulpit I am now serving. If I cite anything from geology, there is professor a, teacher of this science, right before me. If I use an illustration of Roman mythology, there is professor ready to trip me up for my little inaccuracy. If I mention something in English literature that pleases me, I am cowered by the presence of the learned man that teaches that subject. What shall I do?" The sagacious old man replied," Do not be discouraged. Preach the gospel. They probably know very little of that."[39]

A recent study on the competition to preaching, found some competition is outside the church, while others are within the church and even within some preachers. The great increase and availability of books, magazines, newspapers, radio, the motion picture and the instant availability of television are all in competition with the preaching of the word of God. And though these tools challenge the intelligence, freshness, relevance and reality of preaching, and must be utilized for the ends of preaching, they cannot be substituted for it. When God spoke to men he sometimes chose a writer but much more frequently he chose a speaker. The Bible has a preference of go and tell over write and send. Thus the living voice will never be superseded as long as it's a voice and not an echo.

You also have the duties of the minister that can interfere with the preaching of the word. A Christian minister is not only a preacher; a minister is a teacher, pastor, administrator, counselor, community servant, and perhaps other things. This variety of tasks can lead to neglecting the preaching of the word. These tasks are not unimportant and are not to be minimized, but should be given a secondary role. When the apostles encountered this tension between tasks, they decided, it is not desirable for us to neglect the word of God in order to serve tables. These first preachers requested assistance with other duties, delegated responsibility, and said they would devote themselves to prayer and the ministering of the Word. As a result the number of disciples increased greatly.

Still another challenge to the preaching of the word of God may come from within the minister. He may lose faith in preaching, expect no lives to be changed or not see God in the midst of his preaching. Consequently, no salvation or deliverance takes place and the power of God will not be active in the lives of the saints. Not that the word of God will not impact the listener regardless of the orator, but the Bible holds the minister accountable for how the word is ministered.

The word of God has its own intrinsic power. The Bible states that it is sharper than any two edged sword and heaven and earth will pass away, but the word of

God will stand forever. The grass withereth and the flower fadeth, but the word of God will last forever. In the beginning was the word and the word was made flesh and dwelt among us, and the heavens and the earth were framed by the word of God.

Therefore, preaching is always a necessity because it is linked to the life of the church. Only the same proclamation can keep life in the church. For the Bible declares that faith cometh by hearing and hearing by the word of God. So the Lord led me to preach a sermon that emphasized the importance of the word of God.

One of Paul's addresses to the Romans related to the legal relations we have if we violate God's holy law, whether a Christian or an unsaved person. He lets them know that sin separates man from God. Paul then begins to speak about that legal relationship being reversed through believing Jesus Christ. He decrees that if you confess with your mouth the Lord Jesus

Christ and believe he was raised from the dead, thou shalt be saved. Following his discussion on one's legal relationship to God as a law violator and how it is reversed through repentance, he begins to talk about the new life. The new life is the life that results from the conversion. The apostle makes plain that the new life accompanies the change in relationship. Once you make the change, a new life comes with it.

This begs the questions of why people's lives are tore up. Why is there so much failure in the church? Why are the saints going under instead of going over? There is no failure in God, but yet Christians are experiencing failure. Why don't they have the victory? If the new life comes with the change in relationship, how come Christians are not able to endure?

Young women continue to get pregnant when they do not have a husband. Marijuana has control over a three hundred and fifty pound football player who can bench press four hundred pounds. Heroin has taken control over men and men and women have no control over their sexual urges. But yet, people don't want to go to church on Sunday mornings, and live across the country and say that TD Jakes is their pastor. Don't tell me the word of God is not needed when the Christian believes he does not have to attend church, but is constantly experiencing trouble.

What's the problem? Research suggests one of two things. Either there is something wrong with the vessel or something wrong with the person that is supposed to be experiencing change. How is it that people who receive the word of God remain the same? Could it be that individuals receive the word, but as it is being filtered in their minds, something is lost? You will know when new life over takes the Christian because he will be in church, will begin to inquire of the pastor how he can contribute to the ministry, and will begin to that which is acceptable to God.

Have You Heard

The Apostle Paul's ultimate desire was for his people to be saved. He anguished over the fact that they were the chosen people, but yet unbelievers as a nation, and he dreaded their consequences. He asserted that it was not good enough to be zealous. Paul stressed, to verbally say that God knows your heart is not good enough. You have to do things according to knowledge, and demonstrate righteous behavior. He desired salvation for a people who were spiritually blind and rejected Christ.

Just as the Christian of old, today's believers are ignorant of God's righteousness, his justification of their guilt, and his desire to be trusted. Today's believers are seeking to establish their own righteousness, instead of believing the true and living God. In order to believe God, one has got to hear him. Isaiah said, "Lord, who hath believed our report? Where shall one find a believer?" God said to Israel and is saying the same thing to today's Christian, "All the daylong have I stretched out my hand unto a disobedient and gainsaying people." This is a forewarning that in the day that you hear his voice, harden your heart.

Honesty and seriousness in religion, is no excuse, and will not compensate, for the deliberate rejection of saving truth. To blatantly disregard the word of God after hearing the preacher, who has preached his heart out, and not repent, is wrong. The true cause of God's word being rejected is the mind of the individual, which has a false notion of its own. So long as people seek to set up their own righteousness, they will not hear the Lord.

The essential terms of salvation have in every age been the same. Whosoever will is invited to life freely. So, how can you neglect such a great salvation? The question of how shall they hear without a preacher should be a sound that rings in the ear of all churches and church members.

Have You Heard

God is often found by those who are the farthest from him, while he remains undiscovered by those who think themselves the nearest. His dealings even with reprobate sinners are full of tenderness and compassion, all the daylong extending the arms of mercy to the disobedient and gainsaying. This will be felt and acknowledged at last by all who perish. Please attend church on Sunday, hear the word of God and make it practical in your life.

Chapter 29
A Form of Godliness

This know also that in the last days perilous times shall come, for men shall be lovers of their ownselves, covetous, boasters, proud, blasphemers, disobedient to parents, unthankful, unholy, without natural affection, trucebreakers, false accusers, despisers of those that do good, traitors, heady, high-minded, and lovers of pleasure more than lovers of God. Having a form of Godliness but denying the power thereof: from such turn away. For of this sort are they which creep into houses, and lead captive silly women laden with sin, lead away with divers lust ever learning, and never able to come to the knowledge of the truth (2 Timothy 3:1-7).

Shortly after winning the Nobel Peace Prize in 1964, the great Dr. Martin Luther King Jr. gave a speech at Illinois Wesleyan University, that great institution in my backyard. In his speech Dr. King stated, there was a question on the lips of millions of people around the world. The question asked by many was, are we really making any progress in race relations. His answer to a rhetorical question was there are three answers to this question, one is extreme optimism, the second is extreme pessimism and the third is the realist position.

The point that the extreme optimist and the extreme pessimist would agree on is that we can sit down and do nothing, said Dr. King. The extreme optimist would say sit down and do nothing because integration is inevitable. The extreme pessimist would say sit down and do nothing because integration is impossible. The realist would agree with the optimist that we have come a long, long way and also with the pessimist, we have a long, long way to go.[25]

The black man was first brought to this country in 1619, slavery was considered to be ordained by God, and African Americans were treated as less than human. In 1857, in the Dread Scott decision, the Supreme Court, the highest court in the land, ruled that the Negro was not a United States citizen, and was merely property. This decision became known as the Court's worst inflicted

A Form of Godliness

wound for African Americans. The ruling went on to say that the Negro had no rights that the white man was bound to respect. In the 1892 Plessey v. Ferguson case, the Supreme Court ruled that blacks and whites should be separate but equal with strict enforcement of the separate, but without the slightest intention to abide by the equal.[9]

To the credit of black and white folk of that time, they didn't just sit back and take it. Caucasian and African Americans strategized, planned and came up with tactics to fight back. If you read the Plessy v. Ferguson case, you learned that it was a test case challenging the 1890 Louisiana Separate Car Act. It required separate accommodations for blacks and whites on railroads. A group of black, creole and white citizens formed the Committee of Citizens to repeal the law, and persuaded Homer Plessey, a man of mixed race to participate in the orchestrated test case.

Plessey was born a free man and was an Octoroon, seven eighths European descent and one eighth African

A Form of Godliness

American. However, under Louisiana law, he was classified as black and required to sit in the colored car. Plessey bought his first class ticket and the rest is history. The United States Supreme Court voted seven to one with the majority opinion supporting white supremacy. Separate but equal remained law until the 1954 Brown v. Board of Education Supreme Court ruling.[28]

True religion, if we are to be honest, asserts that God loves all people, all people are made in his image, and when he redeemed us, he restored us to his image. The color of a man's skin does not determine his worth, and the texture of a man's hair does not validate his dignity. Wiretapping Dr. King and other African American civil rights leaders was wrong, but everybody is not a racist, as suggested by the Federal Bureau of Investigation's Director James Comey.[8]

African Americans had to sit in the back of the bus, drink from separate water fountains, attend black schools, and were lynched. Blacks are currently over represented in the

A Form of Godliness

court system and unarmed black men are being shot and killed. Don't get it twisted, it's great that Director Comey admits to the FBI's history of racism, but don't try to flip the script and imply that all people including other law enforcement officers are racist because they're not.[31]

If you want to talk hate crime, mass murder, racial supremacy, or terrorism, history tells me that in 1963 it was Addie Mae Collins, Cynthia Wesley, Carol McNair and Carole Robertson who were killed in the Sixteenth Street Baptist Church bombing. Racism was the motivation. Described as one of the most vicious and tragic crimes ever perpetrated against humanity, two of the perpetrators weren't even adjudicated until 2001. So, please don't insult my intelligence, don't tell me it's raining outside when clearly it's snowing.

A person with a form of Godliness is more symbolic than real. This individual is one who is a fraud, phony, fake, spiritually powerless to be kind, loving and caring toward all people. The Bible considers the person to have a form

A Form of Godliness

of Godliness because Godliness is talked about, but not demonstrated. What we as a society have to realize is that the power of God is a necessity to be Godly.

It takes absolutely no power to proclaim that everybody is a little racist. We should not turn our backs on people who are being shot and killed just because of the color of their skin or because they are wearing a police uniform. The Black Lives Matter movement has protesters who want the violence to stop, not escalate and most police officers do too. We didn't turn our backs on Governor George Wallace when he stood for segregation, law makers who have persisted in punishing crack offenders ten times harsher than those who use powder cocaine, nor on the law makers making it harder for black folk to vote.

Think it not strange that the Republican ruled congress confirmed Ash Carter, but purposefully delayed the Loretta Lynch's confirmation. Don't tell me your heart is full of love and you have power with God, but hate

A Form of Godliness

immigrants, and struggle to vote for a woman, when we have been voting for white men all our life.

Two things about the civil rights movement that has always caused me to be taken aback are Dr. King's ability to persevere despite his personal problems and more importantly, the fact that white protesters stood for civil rights even though they had nothing to gain and everything to lose. If I were to give a diversity or black history speech today, the first three people I'd mention are Viola Liuzzo, Reverend James Reeb, and Jonathan Myrick Daniels, my white brothers and sister who were murdered in the civil rights struggle. The aforementioned Caucasian people fought for black people even though they risked being called a nigger lover, bitten by dogs, and being beaten and shot to death, that's love.

Paul instructed Timothy, a young preacher and pastor that he was living in the last days and that perilous times would come. If the last days are defined as a period before the second coming of Christ, that means we are living in that

A Form of Godliness

time. Thus, if you have your right mind, shelter, food and raiment, you had better praise the Lord because difficult times could come upon you at any time.

A form of Godliness is possessed by the person who has no power. Let me make it perfectly clear that if you are standing up for righteousness and get killed, that does not mean you were weak or lacked the power of God. How do I know this to be true? Stephen, Peter, Andrew, Jesus and James are all role models who stood for justice. Stephen was killed for preaching the gospel. Peter and Andrew were crucified. James was put to death by Agrippa and Jesus too was crucified for the sake of righteousness.

Having Godliness means you have self-restraint, control, and piety. Having a form of it means you love the appearance, impression, resemblance, and pretense of Godliness, but you are fronting. With true Godliness come holiness, goodness, faithfulness and denying of self. With a form of it, you are faithless.

A Form of Godliness

The power is necessary for joy, regeneration, and sanctification. Too many people turn away from the power and end up creeping with silly women laden with sin, Paul said. To be laden with sin is to be loaded, weighed down, burdened or overloaded with unrighteousness, becoming easy prey of the devil.

Though the scripture says that women are led away with diver's lust, men can't put it all on the woman because it works both ways. Men know the word, are knowledgeable, informed, but too can be rebellious. Just as sin is pleasurable for a season, men and women are going to get away with it for a period, but there is coming a time when seducing others and the sins of men will no longer be concealed and their form of Godliness will be revealed.

Chapter 30
Power Connection

The Lord said unto Moses, rise up early in the morning, and stand before Pharaoh, and say unto him, thus saith the Lord God of the Hebrews, let my people go, that they may serve me. For I will at this time send all my plagues upon thine heart, and upon thy servants, and upon thy people, that thou mayest know that there is none like me in all the earth. For now I will stretch out my hand that I may smite thee and thy people with pestilence, and thou shalt be cut off from the earth. For this cause have I raised thee up, for to show in thee my power, and that my name may be declared throughout all the earth. Yet exalt thou thyself against my people, that thou wilt not let them go. Behold, tomorrow about this time I will cause it to rain a very grievous hail, such as hath not been in Egypt since the foundation thereof even until now (Exodus 9:13-18).

In his book *Secrets of Spiritual Stamina*, Stuart Briscoe tells the story of a man who bought a new computer. Bringing his new prize home, he carefully opened the box,

Power Connection

gingerly took the machine out, studied its manual, and connected the wires. Eagerly he flipped on the power switch, but nothing happened. Puzzled, the man switched the computer off and rechecked all the connections. He rounded up a screwdriver and fastened the wires more securely. He again read the relevant portion of the manual. Satisfied that he'd followed directions, he flipped the computer on and again nothing happened. As his anger rose, the man's little girl walked into the room. "Hi Daddy!" Her cheery voice rang out. "What a pretty computer! Can I plug it in?"[5]

How does one make it in these last and evil days? How do you survive the persecution of the enemy? How do you fulfill your God given potential when the cares of life can get you down? How can you be victorious in all that you do? How can we combat violence, deal with race relations, and develop good police and community relations and resolve other social ills in society? Well, I'm convinced it is by the power of God. If God be for us, he's more than if the whole wide world is against us. He's the lion of Judah that breaks every chain and gives to us the victory again, again and again. We can't go under for going over; greater is he that is in us than he that is in the world. The righteous have never been forsaken nor his seed begging bread.

Could it be that there is a power outage? I don't know how people are making it without Jesus. The world is dying, but God commended his love toward us, in that, while we were yet sinners, Christ died for us.

Salvation is a prerequisite for the power connection. If all have sinned and come short of the glory of God and sin separates man from God, we have no hope, patience, or ability to be long suffering, loving and caring, without repentance and a committed life. Romans 3:10 says there is none who is righteous, no not one. Therefore, without God we are at a greater risk to be cruel, full of cursing, liars, cheaters, and destructive.

Spiritual Death is the result of unrighteousness. For by grace are we saved through faith and that not of ourselves least any man should boast. By faith we are sitting in heaven with Jesus who is at the right hand of the Father and this hope shall soon become reality.

We are the salt of the earth, but if the salt loses its savor, wherewith shall it be salted? It is thenceforth good for nothing, but to be cast out, and to be trodden under the foot of men. Living Christianity preserves the earth from corruption, freshens and sweetens and is the remedy for racial unrest and all hatred. Christianity's active presence of discipleship exhibits love toward all people, and takes a stand against racist attitudes, feelings and beliefs. The Christian doesn't recoil and become exasperated when dealing with mean spirited people and their behavior. If you don't stand for something you will fall for anything.

If the Christian loses its savor, the world then can't be salted. If we can't be salt unto the world, we are really good for nothing, and might as well not be saved. The focal point is not on whether the salt will have an impact on the person needing to be restored, but on who else can supply the earth with living Christianity except the follower of Christ.

The Lord is not slack concerning his promise as some men count slackness, but is long suffering toward us, not willing that any should perish, but that all should come to repentance. God does not want anyone to be lost and he's waiting on those who don't know him as Lord and savior. Salvation doesn't end with us, and there are many people that the Lord wants to save.

To be long suffering is to wait until the full number of those appointed to salvation is completed. The Christian shouldn't say come now Lord Jesus because there is someone else who wants to hear the Lord say enter in and well done thou good and faithful servant. God is calling others to his kingdom, but they don't know it. He loves the ninety-nine, but is more concerned about the one. I say unto you, that likewise joy shall be in heaven over one sinner that repents, than over ninety and nine just persons, which need no repentance.

Christian people should not get upon themselves as though they have arrived because no one can be the light of the world without God. Your salt and light work like this, salt operates internally and has the greatest impact when it mixes while the sunlight operates externally irradiating all that it touches. Like a city that sits on a hill, your light radiates to the person that you mix with. We are supposed to be mixers and radiators. We must always remember that everyone has some redeeming qualities and Christ's return is being delayed to be gracious to the rebellious and gainsaying.

Six times Moses made the demand to Pharaoh to let God's people go, yet Moses made a seventh plea. God can cause plagues to come upon the heart and body of our enemies making it hopeless for them. Moses proclaims that Pharaoh will become a standing monument of the justice and power of God's wrath. When God judges, he accomplishes what he sets out to achieve and none have ever hardened their heart against God and prospered. If God can create a rebellious person like Pharaoh to show his power, he certainly can use you to show forth his supremacy.

Providence ordered it so that Moses should have a man of such a fierce and stubborn spirit to deal with. God will humble your enemies. Enemies are humbled to show God's unquestionable sovereignty, irresistible power, and his inflexible justice. He sometimes will catapult very bad men to honor and power, spare them long, and suffer them to grow dreadfully disrespectful, that he may be so much the more glorified in their destruction.

But thou shalt remember the Lord thy God, for it is he that giveth thee power to get wealth that he may establish his covenant which he swore unto thy fathers. God wants us to be empowered to have an impact on the world, but there is only one way to gain the power he so desires us to have. Scripture states, but ye shall receive power, after that the

Holy Ghost is come upon you and ye shall be witnesses unto me both in Jerusalem, and in all Judaea, and in Samaria, and unto the uttermost part of the earth. God has commissioned Christians to always show strength in weakness. And he said unto me, my grace is sufficient for thee, for my strength is made perfect in weakness. Most gladly therefore will I rather glory in my infirmities, that the power of Christ may rest upon me.

Conclusion

In conclusion, I want to give you scriptures related to hope. As I've mentioned throughout this book, with hope all things are possible. Love for different races of people, genders, mean spirited neighbors, prejudicial bosses, racist government officials, and murderers is possible with the hope of Christ.

Let me start with reiterating my favorite scripture regarding hope. Ecclesiastes 9:4 states, "For him who is joined to all the living there is hope; a living dog is better than a dead lion." The lion, one of the noblest of animals has no opportunity being dead while the dog symbolic of the vilest of person's being alive still has an opportunity to achieve great things. Remember, anyone amongst the living has hope no matter what they've done, but the noblest that die unconverted have no hope.

The title scripture is actually my second favorite. Proverbs 13:12 states, "Hope deferred makes the heart sick but when the desire comes it is a tree of life." True happiness is attained when you first realize you can have hope. Deferred means that it's late, been postponed, is tardy, but once it shows up it will show out. A happy person is the easiest person to get along with, work with, love and is a giver not a taker. Be of good courage and God shall strengthen your heart, all you that hope in the Lord. Your soul waits for the Lord; he is your help and your shield. He knows the thoughts that he thinks toward you, thoughts of peace, and not of evil, to give you an expected end. Hope makes you not ashamed, because the love of God is shed abroad in your heart by the Holy Ghost. All things work together for your good because you love God, and are called according to his purpose. You through the spirit wait for the hope of righteousness by faith. Rejoice in hope; be patient in tribulation and constant in prayer. They that wait upon the Lord shall renew their strength; mount up with wings as eagles; they shall run, and not be weary; they shall walk and not faint.

Jesus said if thou can believe, all things are possible to him that believes. For we are saved by hope; but hope that man seeth, why doth he yet hope for? If we hope for that we see not, then do we with patience wait for it. Blessed is the man that trusted in the Lord, and whose hope the Lord is. But I will hope continually, and will yet praise the Lord more and more.

We have access by faith into this grace wherein we stand, and rejoice in hope of the glory of God. So, fear thou not; for I am with thee; be not dismayed; for I am thy God; I will strengthen thee; yea, I will help thee; yea, I will uphold thee with the right hand of my righteousness. Now the God of hope fill you with all joy and peace in believing, that ye may abound in hope, through the power of the Holy Ghost.

References

1. Alexander, M., (2012), The new Jim Crow mass incarceration in the age of colorblindness, New York: New York Press.
2. Almasy S. and Catherine S., (2014, May) Magic Johnson in exclusive interview I'm going to pray for Donald Sterling, CNN. Retrieved from http://www.cnn.com/2014/05/13/us/magic-johnson-donald-sterling-interview/index.html.
3. Babwin D., and Tarm, M., (2015, November), Suicide of G.I. Joe cop rocks Illinois town, wife, son are investigated, Nation and World News.
4. Beatty, C., (2013, November), A real life scandal, Essence Magazine. Retrieved from http://www.essence.com/2013/10/11/kwame-Kilpatrick-scandal-Christine-Beatty-essence.
5. Briscoe, S., (2000, March 7), Secrets of spiritual stamina, Charlotte: Billy Graham Evangelistic Association.

6. Borba, M., (2016), UnSelfie: why empathetic kids succeed in our all about me world, New York: Touchstone Press.
7. Broadus J., (1979), On preparation and delivery of sermons, San Francisco: Harper and Row.
8. C-Span, (2015, February 12), Law enforcement and race relations.
9. Cates, D., (2013), Plessey v. Ferguson segregation and the separate but equal policy, Minneapolis: ABDO Publishing Company.
10. Celebrity Crime Files, (2012, October 15), Sam Hurd and Darryl Henley, Season 3 Episode.
11. Change, Web 12 Dec. 2016. Retrieved from http://www.sermonillustrations.com/a-z/c/change.htm.
12. Cheerful Givers, Web 12 Dec. 2016. Retrieved from https://bible.org/illustration/cheerful-givers.
13. Clifford Larson, K., (2004), Harriet Tubman portrait of an American hero, New York: Random House Publishing.

14. Dake, F. J., (1987) God's plan for man, Lawrenceville, Dake Bible Sales Inc.
15. Du Bois, W., Burghardt, E., The souls of black folk, 1868-1963 essays and sketches, Chicago: McClurg & Co.
16. Failures in Ministry, Sermon Illustrations, Web 12 Dec. 2016. Retrieved from http://www.sermonsearch.com/sermon-illustrations/7516/failures-in-ministry/.
17. Franklin, V., (1995), Living our stories telling our truths: autobiography and the making of African American intellectual tradition, New York: Oxford University Press.
18. Elliott, C., (2010) White coat, black hat: adventures on the dark side of medicine, Boston: Beacon Press.
19. Generosity, Biblia.work, Web 12 Dec. 1995. Retrieved from http://www.biblia.work/sermons/generosity/.
20. God wants your inabilities, Bible.org, Web 2 Feb. 2009. Retrieved from

https://bible.org/illustration/god-wants-your-inabilities.
21. Goldstein, J., (2013, August 12), Judge rejects New York's stop and frisk policy, New York Times.
22. Home Safe at Last, Bible.org, Web 2 Feb. 2009. Retrieved from https://bible.org/illustration/home-safe-last.
23. *Illinois General Assembly.* (n.d.), Fornication. Retrieved from http://www.ilga.gov/legislation/ilcs/fulltext.asp?DocName=072000050K11.
24. *Illinois General Assembly.* (n.d.), Adultery. Retrieved from http://www.ilga.gov/legislation/ilcs/fulltext.asp?DocName=072000050K11.
25. King, M., (1966), (Recorded by WJBC), Retrieved from https://www.iwu.edu/mlk/
26. Knowles, B., Thaddis Harrell Terius Nash, and Christopher Stewart, (2008), Put a ring on it. I Am Sasha Fierce. *On Columbia Records*, Burbank, California: The Boom Boom Room.

27. Leber, R., (2014, August 12), Police officers are more likely to shoot black men, studies suggest, The New Republic.
28. *Legal Information Institute.* (n.d.), Plessy v. Ferguson. Retrieved from https://www.law.cornell.edu/supremecourt/text/163/537.
29. Lowery, W., (2016, July 11), Are more white people than black people killed by police? Yes but also no, The Washington Post.
30. Little, G. and Robinson, K. (1997) How to escape your prison, Memphis, Eagles Wing Books, Inc.
31. McGregor, J. (2015, February 13), FBI Director James Comey's unprecedented speech on race, The Washington Post.
32. Moore, B. (2005). *Building Bridges Leadership Training Manual.* Chicago, IL: National Coalition Building Institute.
33. Pastoring, Sermon Illustrations.com, Web July 1994. Retrieved from

http://www.sermonillustrations.com/a-z/p/pastoring.htm.

34. Police officers are more likely to shoot black men studies suggest, Web 12 Aug. 2014. Retrieved from https://newrepublic.com/article/119060/michael-brown-studies-show-racial-bias-police-shootings.

35. Preach the gospel, Pulpit Helps.com, Web 2016. Retrieved from http://www.pulpithelps.com/www/docs/896-3937.

36. Shay, A., (2012), Remembering Ida B. Wells-Barnett, Chapel Hill: University of North Carolina.

37. Sotomayor, S., (2013), My beloved world, (New York: Vintage Books).

38. Straus, M. A., & Gelles, R. J. (1990). Physical violence in American families: Risk factors and adaptations to violence in 8,145 families. New Brunswick, NJ: Transaction.

39. Sundew flower, Our Daily Bread, Web 11 Dec. 1992. Retrieved from https://bible.org/illustration/sundew-flower.

40. Temptation, Sermon Illustrations.com, Web 11 Dec. 1992. Retrieved from http://www.sermonillustrations.com/a-z/t/temptation.htm.
41. Tongue, Sermon Illustrations, Web 27 Jan. 2017. Retrieved from http://www.sermonillustrations.com/a-z/t/tongue.htm.
42. Top Ten New Year's Resolutions, Web 21 July 2016. Retrieved from http://pittsburgh.about.com/od/holidays/tp/resolutions.htm.
43. Turkle, S., (2015), Reclaiming conversation: the power of talk in a digital age, New York: Penguin Press.
44. TV witches popularize occult, Preaching Today. Web Oct. 2009. Retrieved from http://www.preachingtoday.com/illustrations/2001/january/12803.html.

45. Wanshel, E., (2016, July 18) Black lives matter protest becomes bbq and real talk with police, The Huffington Post.
46. Wedding Ceremony, Revolvy, Web 12 Dec. 2016. Retrieved from https://www.revolvy.com/main/index.php?s=Wedding%20ceremony&item_type=topic.
47. When I stand at the judgment seat, Sermon Illustrations, Web 9 Dec. 2016. Retrieved from http://www.sermonsearch.com/sermon-illustrations/3636/when-i-stand-at-the-judgment-seat/.
48. Williams, J., (2008, May 23), McCain rejects controversial pastor's backing, Boston Globe.

Made in the USA
Lexington, KY
25 February 2017